EXPERIENTIAL DRAWING

Robert Regis Dvořák

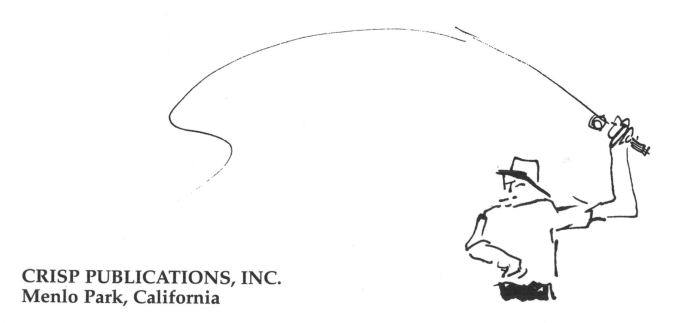

CRISP PUBLICATIONS, INC.
Menlo Park, California

EXPERIENTIAL DRAWING

Robert Regis Dvořák

CREDITS

Editor: Tony Hicks
Design and Composition: R. R. Dvořák
Cover Design: R. R. Dvořák
Artwork: R. R. Dvořák

Printed in the United States of America by Von Hoffmann Graphics, Inc.

CrispLearning.com

00 01 02   10 9 8 7 6 5 4 3 2

Library of Congress Catalog Card Number 91-55519
Dvorak, Robert Regis
Experiential Drawing
ISBN 1-56052-065-5

This book is printed on recyclable paper with soy ink.

Preface

Drawing is a form of self-expression that requires spontaneity, technique, imagination, and skill. Experiential Drawing is a methodology for acquiring this skill quickly and easily.

Drawing is not a competitive sport, though sometimes students consider it so. Nor is it a performance art like dance or music. In this book, drawing is considered a personal experience engaged in for personal reasons.

The purpose of this book is not to teach graphic art, book illustration, or architectural drawing. However, people in these fields may find the book helpful in gaining new skill, increasing enjoyment, or simply loosening up a tight drawing hand.

In this book you are asked to rethink your notions about how drawing is to be approached. Experiential Drawing does not reject drawing techniques; but shifts one's focus away from technique and toward habits for creative expression.

I invented the Experiential Drawing method of teaching in 1976. Since then I have presented this course as a two-day workshop for hundreds of people. I know it works because I have watched students of all ages flower and grow.

This approach to drawing has been overwhelmingly successful. I recall a man who thanked me at the end of a two-day workshop. He said he had a master's degree in fine art and for years had been ashamed because he could not draw. Now he had proven to himself that he could draw, and he knew what he needed to do to strengthen his new confidence. Hundreds of people, of all ages, in my workshops have had serious doubts about even the remotest possibility of success. In only a matter of hours, these doubts were replaced with enthusiasm and excitement.

Experiential Drawing is an attitude, an approach to drawing that will allow you to experience your creativity, increase your visual perception, and participate in spontaneous artistic self-expression. You will become more aware, having moments of personal discovery. The purpose of experiential drawing is not to make perfect drawings, but to bring you closer to your experience. When you do this, the drawings you make will be authentic records of your experience. As your experience becomes richer, the drawings you make will become richer too.

Fear, self-invalidation, and trying hard are the main obstacles to successful drawing. Once these obstacles are dissolved, rapid learning can begin. I have read that we are born with only two fears: the fear of falling and the fear of loud noises. All other fears are learned. By becoming aware of our fears, letting go, and honoring our creative selves we can begin to experience, express, and even inspire ourselves and others with marks on paper. If there is one key to learning to draw it is in the word enjoyment. For, I believe that in *joy* we are *meant* to be.

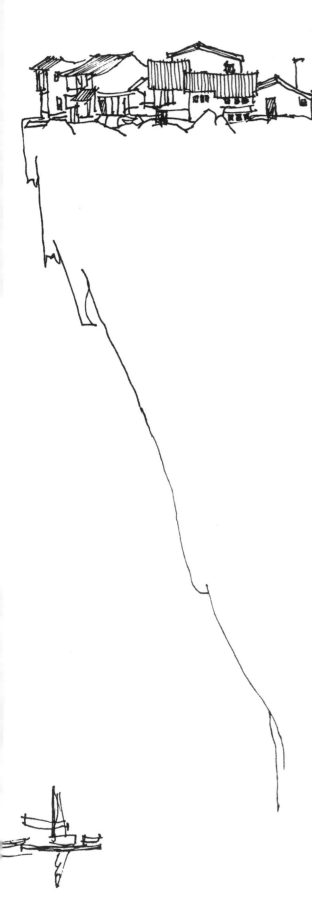

How To Use This Book

Experiential Drawing has been written so you, the reader, can teach yourself to draw. The structured exercises will provide a meaningful experience whether you are a beginner or an advanced student. Read this book with your pen and sketchbook at hand.

As you proceed through the book, don't get frustrated when your drawings do not satisfy your critical eye. Remember that drawing is a process. At first, delay your concern about what is happening on the paper. Decide to enjoy the exploration of your subject. In this way you can avoid the frustrations that come from high expectations. Drawing can be a relaxing and enjoyable activity.

THE EXERCISES

The book has been written so the reader can understand and learn in a step-by-step sequence. Explanations are followed by one or more exercises. These projects call for introspection, risk taking, lack of control, letting go, unusual views, exaggerated perspective, and creative play.

The material has been presented as it would be in a studio class. Whether you consider yourself a beginner or an advanced student, do the written and drawing exercises in sequence. Remember the old Chinese proverb: I hear and I forget, I see and I remember, I *do* and I understand. Keep a wait and see attitude. If you find yourself making deviations from the exercises, consider that also part of your journey.

Remember that learning a new skill requires practice. In learning to play the piano you will strike many wrong keys. The same is true with drawing. Mistakes are part of the program. Trust the process. Its mastery can yield great satisfaction and pleasure.

MATERIALS

BEGINNING MATERIALS

For the first few exercises all you will need is a pen and paper. I recommend a black-ink pen -- a roller-ball pen, a fountain pen, or a felt pen. A sketch book with 9″ x 12″ white paper will be adequate. Later, you will need an 18″ x 24″ pad of white drawing paper and several drawing instruments, described below. I do not recommend pencil yet. It's important to get in the habit of committing your lines to paper without thinking about correcting them.

ADDITIONAL MATERIALS

You will need the following materials to do the exercises in this book:

Bamboo Pen
A bamboo pen with a chisel point is used for more expressive line; thick, thin, dark, and light. You can make your own or buy one and chisel the point with a sharp knife or nail clippers.

Bamboo Stick
A bamboo stick is also great for making expressive lines. It demands an attitude of letting go because of the many surprises it brings.

Calligraphy Pen
A calligraphy dip pen will give you opportunities for making controlled thin and bold lines with the same pen. A good drawing nib to begin with is a Speedball No. B5.

Fountain-Pen Ink
A fountain-pen ink will not damage your pens or brushes. My favorite is the Higgins Non-waterproof Fountain Pen India Ink. You can apply water to this ink even after it has dried and pull lines into beautiful warm grey washes.

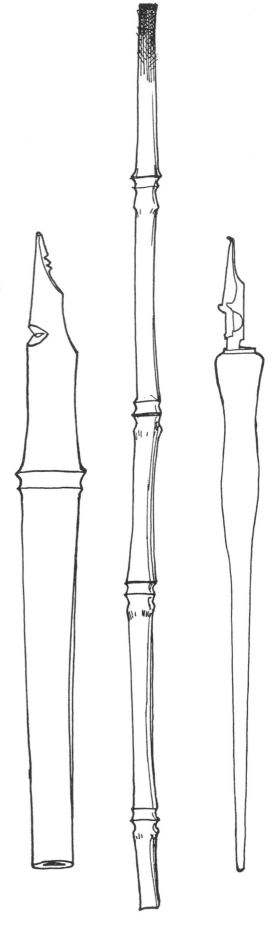

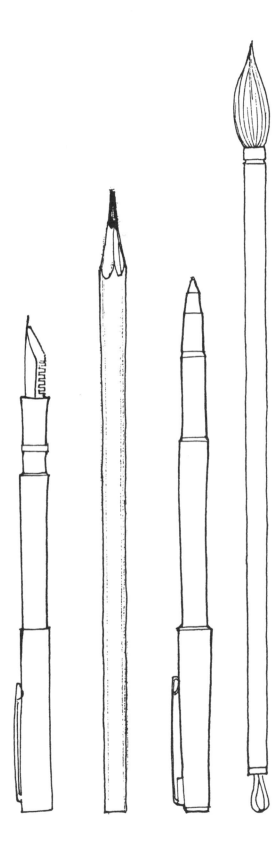

Mixing Dish
A plastic or china saucer can be used as an ink-wash mixing dish.

Paper
I recommend a white drawing paper with some texture. Use a paper that can hold up to the wet ink and pen scraping. For size, I recommend 18" x 24". If you are in a large class and tight on room you can work with 14" x 17". However, the larger size is better. Newsprint is all right, but I prefer a better quality paper. Newsprint tears easily, yellows quickly, and is too absorbent for ink and wash work.

Pen with Fine Nib
A fountain pen with a fine point makes a good all-around drawing instrument. A steel bowl pointed extra fine nib dip pen will also work and is less expensive (my favorite nib is Hunt No. 512). These pens are used for fine line variations.

Pencil
My favorite all-around drawing pencil is the Faber Castell Design Ebony Jet Black Extra Smooth 6325; but a No. 1 wooden writing pencil will work.

Rag
Keep a rag handy for drying the brush and pens.

Roller-Ball or Felt-Tipped Pen
A roller-ball or felt tipped pen is used for consistent, even lines.

Water
Water is needed to make washes and to keep your brush clean.

Watercolor Brush
Use a watercolor brush or Chinese brush of medium size for doing water and ink washes and dry brush work.

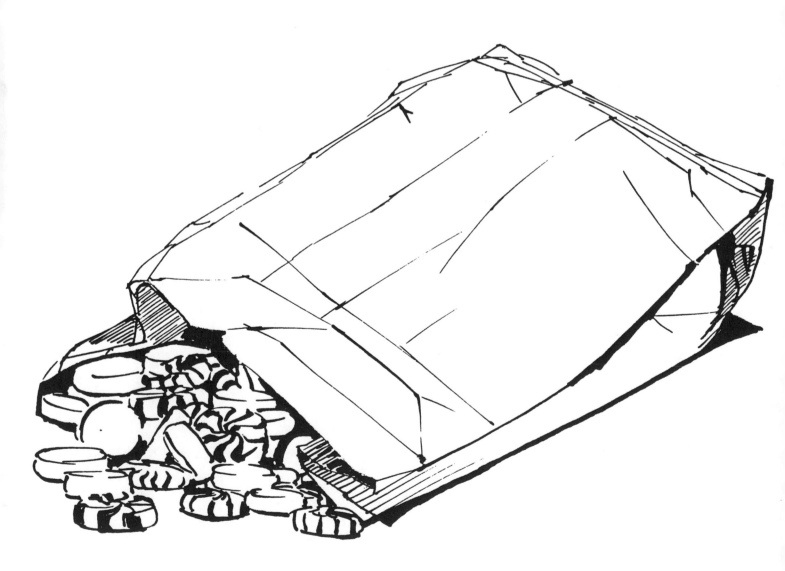

CONTENTS

x

PART I

THE PRINCIPLES

When we experience drawing as a *process of seeing* and not as an attempt to reproduce reality, we express our personal creative vision authentically and effortlessly. The first four chapters will acquaint you with an experiential approach to drawing.

Every great building needs a strong foundation. So too, we must begin on a sure footing. If you are reading this book to learn to draw, read the text and do the exercises outlined in the next four chapters in sequence to establish your footing. And remember, these principles can carry over to other areas of your life as well.

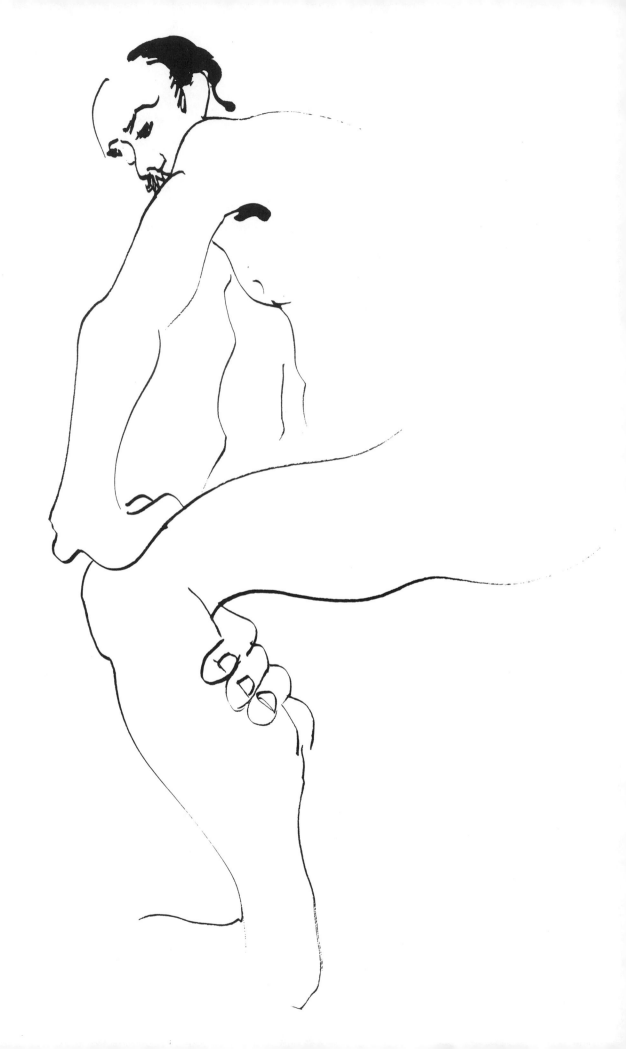

2

1

What Is Experiential Drawing?

Some years ago I was making an extended tour of Europe, doing caricatures in various places to help pay travel expenses. One night in a small cafe in Copenhagen, Denmark, an elderly gentlemen called me over and asked me, "Would you do a caricature of that young woman sitting across the room from me?" I complied with his request. He paid me for the drawing, and asked me to present it to the young woman. He then invited me to sit with him and enjoy a glass of beer. I agreed, and very quickly our conversation turned to philosophical matters. At one point he asked, "What do you think is the most important moment in your life?"

I thought I knew the answers to most questions. I searched my brain. Perhaps it was my birth, for I wouldn't be here if that hadn't occurred. Maybe it will be my death. Or perhaps it will be when I get married, have my first child, reach the age of 40. It could be many moments of importance. I said, "Please tell me," and he answered, "The most important moment in your life is right now."

It is so true. Now is our most important moment for it is the only time we are alive, present, and able to be, do, or have anything. Carlos Castaneda said it so well in his book *Tales of Power*. "Your point of power is now." It is only now that we have the power to do anything.

THE APPROACH

Experiential Drawing focuses on careful observation and personal discovery rather than on technical rules. It encourages spontaneity and builds confidence in one's drawing ability quickly and naturally. Since Experiential Drawing emphasizes the *experience* of drawing, the resulting images become less important. The process is more important than the product. The drawings that result are the evidence of that process.

Each person has a personal signature when writing their name. And so too with drawing. Learning to draw through rules or techniques can be confusing and inhibit our freedom. **Trying to bring about a change will slow down the accomplishment of that change.** It is more important to enthusiastically observe and faithfully record that experience on paper. The marks we make on paper represent our personal awareness and creativity.

THE STRATEGY

We do our best drawings when we are relaxed. When attention on the outcome of the drawing becomes more important than seeing, we lose our concentration. Anxiety over poor results causes tension and frustration and diminishes our ability to observe accurately. The whole process of observation and recording breaks down, and drawing becomes frustrating—instead of relaxing and fun.

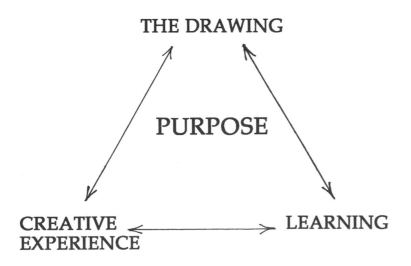

THE DRAWING

PURPOSE

CREATIVE EXPERIENCE

LEARNING

The above diagram shows the strategy of drawing experientially. When we put our attention on our creative experience—the seeing, discovering, feeling process—then learning is fast. The more we learn, the more exciting the creative experience becomes. As the learning process and the creative experience reinforce each other, the resulting drawing will become richer. A discriminating eye will see a true expression of that experience represented in the drawing.

CROSSING THE MAGIC LINE

As you work through this book, you may think that some of the exercises are strange, funny, or even foolish. Experiential Drawing doesn't have to make sense. To draw, we don't even have to think much. But we do need to observe, experience, and create. The act of drawing is like crossing an imaginary line—a magic line. A line that separates rational thinking and creative expression.

EXPERIENCE

(creative expression, spontaneity, nonjudgmental seeing, observation, Experiential Drawing)

<u>an imaginary line</u>   <u>a magic line</u>

RATIONAL THINKING

(judgment, reason, critical thought, analysis)

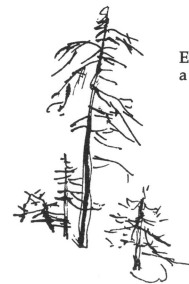

Experiential Drawing is not a matter of knowing, but a matter of doing.

Calligraphy pen sketch of a temple at
Tanjore, India ll" x 8 1/2"

6

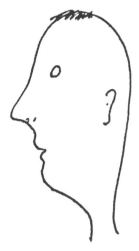

Profile of a man made by an adult student at 9:00 AM–the beginning of a one-day workshop 14" x 11"

Profile of the same man made by the adult student at 2:00 PM the same day 14" x 11"

The drawings above have been proportionately reduced in size.

2

Building a Strong Foundation

An important first step in the Experiential Drawing process is building a foundation for what is to come. In this chapter you will organize your attitudes and get mentally set for what is to follow. Attitude is always more important than aptitude. With the right attitude you will be committed to your task and success will be assured.

THE BENEFITS

Motivation to do something is in proportion to the benefits. The more benefits, the greater the commitment. The purpose of drawing is much more than to make drawings. Here are some of the wonderful benefits.

The most important benefit, especially for students, is the higher self-esteem that comes from accomplishing something marvelous. Truly, the making of a drawing can be a marvelous experience. There is a mystique around drawing. A person who draws is considered by those that don't as a kind of magician. An artist drawing in public always "draws" a crowd. People watch with fascination as the drawing evolves. When I demonstrate drawing for elementary, high school, or adult classes the students watch with rapt attention.

Drawing develops concentration. This is especially valuable with children who are having difficulty staying on task in school. When they learn to concentrate on drawing, it can carry over into their other subject areas. The process of drawing holds our attention in the present, which is an energizing place to be.

The act of seeing and drawing increases visual perception, which will continue even when you are not drawing. People who draw claim to be keenly perceptive and visually aware of their world. When you expand your ability to experience your world you begin to really see the faces of people you talk to. You notice the beauty of the landscape. In short, you become visually aware.

Drawing is a mode of communication. You can express yourself and your view of the world through drawing.

Drawing can help you to discover your creativity.

Drawing is linked directly or indirectly to every manufactured item. Indeed, almost everything man made—buildings, cars, machines, clothes— from skyscrapers to microchips—began with a drawing.

The process of Experiential Drawing is relaxing and energizing.

Experiential Drawing will sharpen the mind's eye. You will develop the ability to imagine and create images in your mind.

We must not forget that we create great satisfaction when we accomplish something we have never done before.

EXERCISE 2-1

Benefit List
There are many benefits for you. Think of as many as you can, and list them in your sketchbook. Include those mentioned, if applicable. Add additional benefits you become aware of as you study. Here are some questions to ask yourself. Write your answers in your sketchbook.

1. What can drawing do for me?

2. What can drawing change for me?

3. How am I going to be able to use drawing?

4. What can drawing teach me?

5. How can drawing help me grow?

EXERCISE 2-2

Reasons You Can Draw
Take all the reasons you think you cannot draw the way you would like to, and rewrite them in your sketchbook as statements that serve your purpose—learning to draw, or to draw with greater skill, spontaneity, etc. It is not necessary that you actually believe what you write. Just do the exercise and be aware of how it feels.

Here are some examples of reasons listed as positive statements.

- I can learn to draw whether I think I have talent or not.
- When it comes to drawing, I can be good.
- I'm getting instruction and learning.
- I practice every day.
- I'm loose and free when I draw.
- I needn't be afraid of criticism.
- I always accept the way it comes out, because that was my experience at that time.
- I can draw just as well as other people can.
- My sister or brother were always good at it. Now I can be an artist in the family too.
- I am going to take the time.
- I have confidence.
- I now know what to do.
- Everyone has imagination.
- I can be very creative.
- I now know how to begin.
- I needn't believe the negative statements of others about my own abilities.

ATTITUDES

Now look at your attitudes about drawing. The first step to eliminating the beliefs that sabotage success is to find out what they are.

Here is a list of reasons people give for not being able to draw as they would like.

- I don't have any talent.
- When it comes to drawing, I'm just no good.
- I've never had any instruction.
- I don't practice enough.
- I'm too tight.
- I'm afraid of criticism.
- It never comes out the way I want it to.
- Other people can all draw better than I can, so what's the use.
- My sister or brother are good at it in our family.
- I don't have the time.
- I don't have any confidence.
- I just don't know what to do.
- I don't have any imagination.
- I'm not very creative.
- I don't know how to begin.
- A teacher in school discouraged me or told me that I can't draw.

Changing Attitudes

We can change our beliefs. Usually it happens when our experience is not consistent with our opinion. Another way to change is to just choose another opinion. When you discover that a certain belief is blocking progress, the best way to unblock yourself is to change the belief.

GOALS AND PURPOSES

All achievements results from well-defined goals and purpose. There is no point in taking aim unless there is a target. If you aim at nothing, you get nothing. The last step in our foundation construction is to establish concrete goals. Don't be timid when you make them. I have seen some incredible results from people who dared to "shoot for the moon."

EXERCISE 2-3

Your Goals
List your goals on a new page in your sketchbook. Ask yourself: What will be required to feel really good about my drawing ability? What is my purpose for drawing? What do I want to accomplish?

Design your outcomes. While you are writing goals, you may want to list other goals that don't have anything to do with drawing.

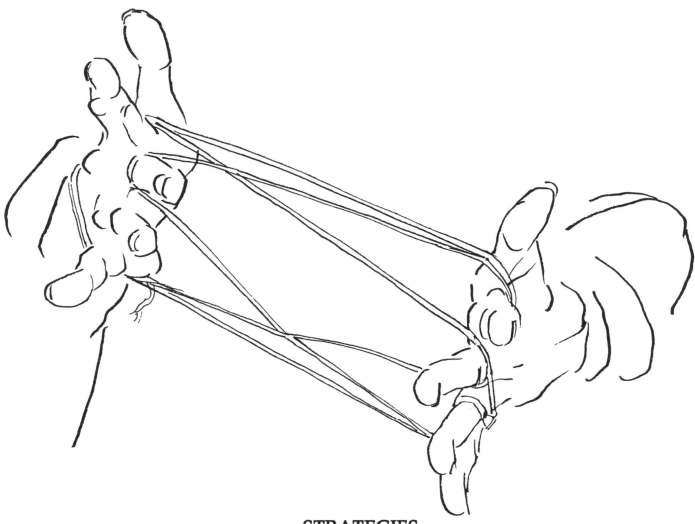

STRATEGIES

Once you know what your goals are, you can decide what you need to do to reach them—what you need to change, what you need to learn, and what you need to unlearn.

EXERCISE 2-4

Your Strategies
The next step in building your foundation is to write down all the strategies that occur to you. What do you think you need to do to be able to draw the way you want to? For example, you might write:

1. I must learn to see better.

2. I need to relax and let go.

3. I have to learn techniques.

4. I need some lessons.

On a new page in your sketchbook list all the things you need to do.

RESPONSIBILITY

The exercises in this chapter are designed to help you take responsibility for your experience in drawing. They are essential for learning to draw experientially. In taking responsibility for your own experience and your drawings, you need to give up a lot of your favorite villains. They might be parents, friends, teachers, or conditions that seem to be beyond your control.

The more responsibility you are willing to take for your experience, the higher your self-esteem will be. And self-esteem is the mainspring for successful learning.

Continuous line eye and nose study
made with the roller ball pen
Actual size 2 minutes

3

Becoming Competent

When you begin to draw it is important that you feel you are capable of the task. Approaching a drawing with insecurity and fear seldom works. In the previous chapter you established a strong foundation. You have prepared yourself mentally and motivated yourself to begin. Now you are going to generate confidence and competence.

YOUR POINT OF POWER

There is only one time and one place that experience can occur. That is here and now. To be competent we must be attentive to what is happening here and now.

An essential principle of Experiential Drawing is that you become *aware* of your experience as you draw. Pay attention to the subject you are seeing and the feelings you are having about that subject. Notice in a non-judgmental way the lines you are making. Listen to the sound of the pen. Feel the texture of the paper under your drawing instrument.

Give yourself enough room to work. Clean off your table and have only what you need in front of you—your pen and sketchbook. Put the cap on the back of the pen for added length and balance. Hold the pen easily, near the middle, or even further back if you like. Don't hold the pen down near the point as you do when you write.

> "Oh you may be sure that Columbus was happy—not when he had discovered America but when he was discovering it ... It's life that matters, nothing but life—the process of discovering, the everlasting and perpetual process."
>
> —Fyodor Dostoevsky, *The Idiot*

IMAGINATION BLOCK

Certain misconceptions can block progress. One is the idea that "I don't have any imagination." Of course, this is not true. We all have imagination.

We all use our imagination many times every day. Our activities are first created in the imagination. When you go to a movie, you plan your trip in your imagination before you leave home. When you prepare a meal, you plan it in your imagination first.

Have you ever looked at the clouds and seen shapes and figures in them? It's your imagination that does that.

When we draw, we plan what we are going to do before we begin. And we continue to use our imagination to explore and discover during the process.

TALENT BLOCK

Another misconception is the idea that "I don't have any talent." Many people believe you are either born with drawing ability or you are not. But were you born with driving skill or typing skill or baseball skill or cooking skill? Were you born walking and talking? Drawing is a skill that can be learned like any other.

People who are good at drawing have drawn a lot. They have practiced and learned. Ask anyone who draws what their first drawings looked like.

Don't let the belief that drawing needs a special talent get in your way. If you can hold a pen and make marks with it, you can draw. I have had thousands of people in my workshops and have never known anyone who could not learn how to draw.

I know, you say you are different. Nonsense! If you are reading this book you already have the most important characteristic of all, *a desire to learn*.

EXERCISE 3-1

Easy Scribble
Visualize your paper with a continuous line that wanders over the paper in every possible direction. You may call it scribbling if you like. Move your pen in the air over the paper without touching it, as if you are making these lines with ease and confidence. See the page well scribbled in your mind's eye.

Now actually make the lines you just visualized. Pay attention that you don't change your hold on your pen. Keep your drawing hand and arm off the paper. Your arm moves freely guiding the pen.

It is not necessary to make any pattern or to organize your scribbles. Just relax and fill up the page with every conceivable movement you can invent. Have fun. When the page is fairly dense with lines, stop.

Later, when you begin to draw subjects, continue to hold and move your pen in the same easy, free way.

SEEING BLOCK

A third misconception is the idea that we all see the same. We don't. There are at least as many ways to see—and draw—as there are people.

Seeing is largely a mental process. The information comes in through the eye, but the brain must process it before we see anything. Our brain selects certain information and filters out other information. To a great extent, we see what we want to see and we don't see what we don't want to see. What we notice depends upon what we are looking for.

If we all see and notice different information, it follows that we will all draw differently. No one can see the way you do. Therefore, no one will ever draw the way you do. Celebrate that idea!

EXERCISE 3-4

Directed Seeing
Walk around the room looking for the following things. Do one at a time.

1. Notice all the color blue you can see.
2. Find all the brown in the room.
3. Discover all the rectangular shapes in the room.
4. Notice all the curved shapes in the room.
5. What are the largest items in the room?

What you did with this exercise is direct your seeing. When you draw experientially, you do the same thing. You direct your visual experience and draw what you find.

EXERCISE 3-2

Using Your Imagination
Look at the scribble drawing you just made. Discover any images you can find in the lines. Look for faces, animals, objects. See how many you can find. Make them stand out by adding lines or darkening the existing lines. If you have difficulty at first, stay with it. Look for large images and small ones. Turn your paper upside down or sideways. Enjoy your exploration. You can even imagine you are looking at a jungle with animals hidden in the bushes.

EXERCISE 3-3

Line Expressions
With your black-ink pen make lines on your paper that express excitement. Don't try to draw any images. Just let the pen move with spontaneous enthusiasm. See how it feels to do this. Delight in messing up the paper. Enjoy doing what you please with your lines. Feel your energy.

GETTING EXCITED

You can get hooked on drawing. But an addiction that puts you in touch with your world, that validates your creative power, that lets you express yourself authentically can't be bad. Ask anyone who loves to draw and you will find out that drawing is a worthwhile pursuit just for the pleasure and satisfaction it brings. I hope you are excited, because that enthusiasm will help you draw with spontaneity and expression.

4

Being Creative

Drawing is a creative activity. To express your creative self requires a creative attitude. In this chapter you will learn what it takes to establish a creative approach. You will also learn how to deal with internal and external distractions.

When we draw experientially we must become courageous in taking risks, making choices, and communicating truthfully. As an adult, regain the attitude of exploration and discovery that you had as a child. Encourage yourself to be resourceful and inventive.

Criticism
Our attitudes about drawing were often formed early. In elementary school children already compare and criticize drawings: "Gee, you're good," or "That looks silly." Such remarks, made to us when we were growing up, may still influence us to like drawing or avoid it.

One woman in her early forties was convinced she could not draw. She explained that when she was in grade school she showed some of her drawings to her mother and father. Her well-meaning parents looked at them and said, "That's okay dear, we can't draw either."

Another woman told me that when she was in elementary school her teacher asked for a drawing of Little Red Riding Hood going to see her grandmother. She produced the drawing and was immediately criticized for the length of the hem on Little Red Riding Hood's dress.

A man remembered being given a drawing assignment to do at home. When he turned it in his teacher punished him because she thought, incorrectly, that an adult must have done the assignment for him.

These three incidents produced blocks that ended further interest in drawing. I have heard many stories like these. If you have a similar story, just remembering the events and recounting them to someone who will listen is usually enough to nullify their effect.

But not everyone who doesn't draw has a story. Most people just stopped drawing in elementary school to concentrate on academic skills—and they never started drawing again. Many people who take up drawing as adults start off drawing as they did at age six or seven. Their drawings are wonderfully naive and childlike.

What we say to ourselves, our children, and our fellow students must be geared to encourage rather than discourage. But be careful, sometimes saying a drawing is good can be just as detrimental as saying it's bad. Before offering *any* words of encouragement read Chapter 13.

External criticism comes from others. Internal criticism comes from ourselves. Both kinds of criticism can block our creativity. Drawing experientially is a process. It requires awareness, attention, and concentration. But criticism is rarely given about our process. Usually it refers to the end result of our process, the lines on the paper. We can avoid internal and external criticism by maintaining our awareness during the drawing process.

EXERCISE 4-1

Shoe Drawing
Make a drawing of a shoe observing carefully each detail. Pay attention to the shapes, the way the laces lay on top of each other, the thickness of the materials, and the stitching.

1

2

3

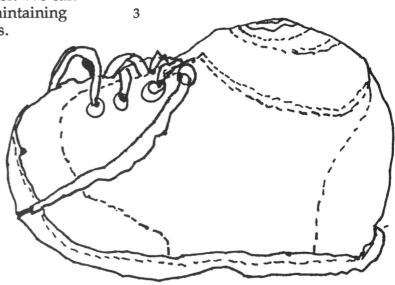

These three drawings were made by Olivia Cheriton, grade 1, age 6, on 9" x 12" drawing paper with a black felt pen during a 45 minute drawing class.

CREATIVITY

Creativity is energizing. It is exciting to make something new, to explore with your mind, eyes, and hands. That is why drawing can be such an exhilarating experience.

If you try too hard and work too hard, you may feel tired. When we are tired we don't feel creative. Maintain a creative attitude and you will feel energized and competent.

When my son David was five he asserted: "I never make *missnakes*."

Everyone makes mistakes. They are part of the learning process. Mistakes are the stepping stones to accomplishment. They allow you to hone and correct constantly.

Mistakes can also be opportunities for creative expression. Let your mistakes show. Let them be part of the process. Let them take you into new directions for expression.

EXTERNAL DISTRACTIONS

Body discomforts—hunger, pain, headache—will distract you from your purpose. So will other people's activities, such as eating, drinking, and talking. Anything that requires override—working in spite of the distraction—will interfere with your awareness.

First, eliminate as many distractions as you can. Then, if there are distractions you can't control, find creative ways to incorporate them into your drawing process. For example, perhaps you can hear someone talking. Instead of upsetting yourself because they are making it difficult to concentrate, draw with the same rhythm the sound of their voices makes.

These three drawings were made by Owen Ellickson, grade 3, age 8, on 9" x 12" drawing paper with a black felt pen during a 45 minute drawing class.

1

2

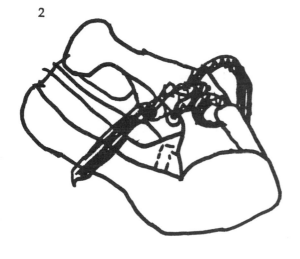

3

INTERNAL DISTRACTIONS

Internal distractions come from your own thoughts, telling you to try harder, warning you not to make mistakes, or simply telling you that you can't draw.

Trying

Trying will rob you of your creative energy. The harder you try, the less satisfying your experience will be. You will only frustrate yourself, become tense and anxious, and eventually get a headache, back pain, or stiff neck.

> *Trying fails, awareness cures.*
> —Fritz Perls

Trying comes from self-doubt. The best way to let go of trying is to become aware of what you are doing. Go through your body and find where you are holding on tight. Breathe deeply, sigh, and surrender to the process. When you trust the process, there is no need to try.

Hesitation

Hesitation occurs when you are indecisive. Pausing often, starting over many times, retracing lines, and chicken scratching are all symptoms of insecurity.

When you are feeling creative and inventive you don't need to hesitate. You proceed with confidence. You draw with certainty. Remember the three D's: be distinct, deliberate, and definite. If you are not certain, pretend you are.

Fritz Perls, in his book *Gestalt Psychology Verbatim*, says, "If we don't know if we will get applause or tomatoes we hesitate, the heart begins to race and all the excitement can't flow into activity, and we have stage fright. So, the formula of anxiety is very simple: anxiety is the gap between the *now* and the *then*. If you are in the now you can't be anxious because the excitement flows immediately into ongoing spontaneous activity. If you are in the now you are creative, you are inventive. If you have your senses ready, if you have your eyes and ears open like a very small child, you find a solution."

BELIEVING IN YOURSELF

We tend to accept only information that confirms our opinions or beliefs. We disregard information that disagrees with our beliefs. If you believe you can't draw, you will tend to notice things that confirm that belief. But you can change your beliefs. Many people prove to themselves that they can draw, by drawing enough times that there is no longer any doubt.

The best approach is to be skeptical of one's beliefs. Accept the idea that whatever your beliefs about drawing may be, they might not be true. This is one belief that is worth believing. It will transform your attitude and open up the possibility for a change in perception.

Trusting in yourself, your creativity, and your ability to learn a new skill will put you in the driver's seat. With these strong attitudes you are in charge of your experience.

1

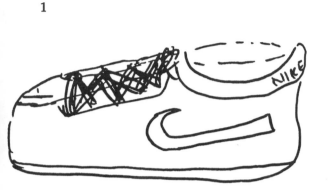

2

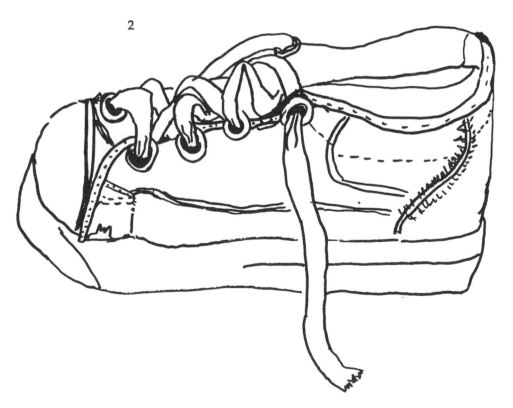

These two drawings were made by Elli Sandis, grade 6, age 11, on 9" x 12" drawing paper with a black felt pen during a 45 minute drawing class.

Model study with ink, dry brush, and
wash 23" x 17" 10 minutes

22

PART II

THE APPLICATIONS

When a child is learning to walk, he or she will take a step or two and then fall. The child then gets up and begins again. Stepping, falling, getting up, and stepping again is the process of learning. The child knows, somehow, that it can learn to walk. When the child falls, he or she does not say, "Oh, I'll never learn this," and quit. No, with enthusiasm and joy he or she continues -- and eventually walks.

Much of our education is based on information gathering. But Experiential Drawing can only be learned by doing. It is not enough simply to read and think about it. Books and teachers will not necessarily have answers for you. To learn, you must engage yourself with the process.

There is a Zen saying, "Right practice furthers." In this part of the book a specific sequence of exercises is outlined. They will give you the opportunity to practice and begin to become aware of your experience. At the same time you will be given the step-by-step coaching you need to draw with joy and skill.

5

Body and Mind Awareness

The basis for Experiential Drawing is self-awareness. This is the *key* that will unlock your creative experience and help you build your skill. The more willing you are to become aware, the faster you will learn. To keep yourself aware, write down what your experience has been after each drawing. This way you will establish the habit of becoming conscious of your experience each time you draw.

BODY POSTURE

It is important to maintain good posture from the beginning. Learn to sit or stand straight, maintaining the natural curvature of the spine. Keep your body balanced and relaxed. The more balanced you are, the less energy it takes to sit or stand. With good posture you will be more alert and will not tire so quickly.

Posture reflects our mental set. Poor posture can reflect psychological insecurity and self-doubt. When you sit or stand straight and tall you will feel better about yourself and have more confidence as you draw.

Relaxation
If you are trying too hard and are worrying about how your drawings look, then drawing will only make you tense and uncomfortable. Keep your body and mind relaxed as you draw. Go through the following exercise from time to time.

Letting Go
Read these instructions first. Sit straight in your chair with your hands resting in your lap and your eyes closed. Now beginning with the top of your head, mentally travel down through your body, making a mental inventory the places where you are tense. As you discover these areas, consciously let go. Tension frequently is located in the eyes, back of the neck, the jaw, the shoulders, the abdominal area, the hands, and the toes. One way to relax these areas is to imagine your breath is penetrating those tight places in your body. Breathe relaxation into these areas. Exhale your tensions.

THE MIND

The mind and the body are one. When the mind is relaxed, the body will follow. When the body is relaxed, the mind will follow. Many people think that the mind is located in the brain. Instead, think of your mind as being everywhere in your body. It is in your eyes, hands, and feet. The hand that records what the eye sees is all part of the same mind. The conscious mind thinks and decides, and the unconscious mind obeys and responds.

Draw From Your Center
Most people imagine that their drawing ability originates in their head or brain—that it is something you know and learn, that it is largely a mental process. The martial arts, such as Karate and Tai Chi, teach the power of focusing the *ki*—the power of our will. Martial art masters practice for years to focus this energy with clear, concentrated purpose.

It is believed that this energy originates in the solar plexus—a network of nerves in the abdomen behind the stomach. Physical activities such as dancing, walking, running, and other sports are best performed from this center of the body. Drawing is also a physical activity. Get the idea that your drawing activity originates from your center, your solar plexus. From here, mentally focus clear, concentrated, creative energy as you draw.

EXERCISE 5-2

Deep Breathing
Oxygen affects the life of every cell in your body. Before beginning to draw, give your system a full oxygen treat with deep diaphragmatic breathing.

1. Exhale all your air through your mouth so you can begin with a fresh supply of air.

2. Relaxing your stomach and lower diaphragm, let the air inflate the diaphragm from the bottom up, breathing in through the nose.

3. Continue to inhale and feel your rib cage expand as your lungs fill. Be careful not to draw your diaphragm inward.

4. After you have inhaled completely, exhale slowly through your mouth. Control the flow of air so it does not come rushing out. Relax your chest and rib cage while you exhale.

5. Finally, pull your diaphragm in to empty all the air. Be careful not to slouch forward as you do this. Now you are ready to repeat the sequence.

Do your breathing exercise at a slow pace. The exhale is usually twice as long as the inhale. Deep breathing can be done sitting or lying down. To enhance the process, close your eyes and become aware of your body breathing.

BREATHING

A common habit is to hold our breath while drawing. We fall into the trap of trying hard and wanting to succeed. We hold our body still to prevent mistakes. If we deprive the body of air by holding our breath, we can soon begin feeling anxious, frustrated, even irritable. Our relaxed body quickly becomes tense.

Breathing is an important part of the drawing process. It is often necessary to remind ourselves consciously to breathe. Put a sign above your drawing board reminding you to breathe, write "breathe" on the front of your sketch book. If you draw with friends, remind each other to breathe often. It will do wonders for your disposition and drawing skill.

BEING GROUNDED

In the martial arts we learn the importance of having the body balanced with the feet firmly on the floor. Ground your body mentally and physically. Plant your feet on the floor. Imagine that you are connected with the earth before you begin to draw. Working with your legs crossed, slouching, sitting, or standing with an unbalanced posture weakens your creative energy flow. Check your body from time to time until you establish the habits outlined above.

Blind contour drawing made for a class
demonstration—33" x 27", one minute.

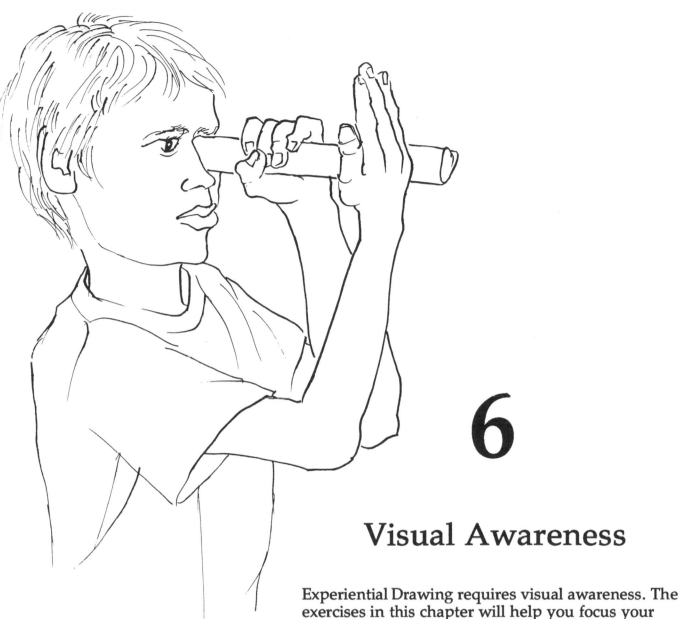

6

Visual Awareness

Experiential Drawing requires visual awareness. The exercises in this chapter will help you focus your vision to perceive as many details of your subject as possible. Watch for the subtle changes in the contours. Investigate your subject like a detective. Don't leave anything unnoticed. The more you explore, the more interested you will become in your subject. And the more interested you become, the more interesting your drawings will be.

BINOCULAR VISION

When we see with two eyes, we see two different images. The brain assembles these into one three-dimensional picture. If you try to draw a subject that is too close to you, you will have difficulty because the view from one eye is noticeably different than the view from the other.

EXERCISE 6-1

Binocular Vision Demonstration
Roll up a sheet of typing paper to make a tube 1¼" in diameter. Hold the tube to your left eye with your left hand, so that you see through the tube with your left eye. Place your right hand against the tube with your palm facing you. Keeping your right eye open, look through the tube with your left eye and focus on whatever you can see through the circle of the tube. Now bring the visual experience of both eyes together. You will seem to see a hole in the palm of your right hand. Binocular vision is the reason for this illusion.

SEEING WITH YOUR NOSE

I recommend using an imaginary nose pencil. This technique takes your attention away from *trying* to see, and at the same time improves your visual perception. It eliminates some of the effort from drawing. It helps improve your vision naturally.

Centralization

The eye sees best at a small point on the retina about the size of a pin head called the *fovea centralis*.

Putting your sight line directly into the fovea centralis is called centralization. At the fovea, vision is 20/20. Just ten degrees off the fovea, vision is reduced to 20/400, which is within the realm of legal blindness. The nose pencil helps direct sight to the fovea centralis. As you nose-pencil your subjects you will automatically be centralizing as you draw.

Relaxation

Using the nose pencil keeps your head moving. This head movement will help keep your neck and shoulders relaxed. You will be amazed at how this technique relaxes those muscles and the muscles that control the eyes. Using the imaginary nose pencil will keep you relaxed all day long whether you are drawing or not. Make it a habit to draw contour lines with your nose pencil.

EXERCISE 6-2

The Nose Pencil Technique
Imagine that you have an imaginary pencil that extends from your nose to the exact point of your visual attention. The pencil goes wherever your interest goes. It can stretch to the farthest point your eye can see and can shrink to the closest point.

When you finish reading this paragraph, look around the room with your imaginary nose pencil. As you discover objects in the room, move your nose pencil around the contours of the objects as if you are drawing them. Do this with several objects at different distances. Notice that your head will move as you trace the object.

Now do the same with the words you are reading. Notice that your head moves back and forth along the lines as you read with your nose pencil. Most of us have the habit of holding our head still. Get in the habit of keeping your head moving as you draw. Guide your nose pencil to find and follow the lines of your subject.

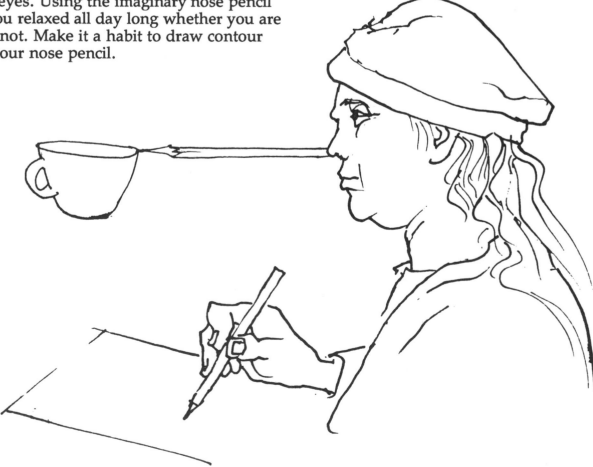

EXERCISE 6-3

Blind Contour Drawing
This exercise is very important and must be done correctly. Read the entire instructions before attempting it. Open your sketchbook to a clean page. If you are working on a single sheet of paper instead of in a sketch book, tape your paper down on the table so it will not move around. Find a place where you will be undisturbed.

You will be drawing your hand. If you hold your pen in your right hand, draw the left hand. If you hold your pen in your left hand, draw the right hand. Lay your hand on the table, far enough away from the paper so you won't be tempted to glance at the paper. Look at your paper and imagine a line-contour drawing on it that will fill the sheet. Draw as large as your paper will allow. Always draw larger than life if you can. If will encourage you to be loose, free, and uninhibited.

Blind contour is done with one continuous line. Before you begin, locate the pen on the paper in the position where you want to start drawing and then move your attention off the paper to your subject—your hand. Carefully follow around the contours of your hand with your eyes or your nose pencil. Let your pen record each variation, each change, as if it is an automatic recording device. Don't look at your paper to see how you are doing. Imagine the point of your pen and your eyes are connected. A good way to do this is to imagine the pen is actually touching your subject as you draw.

Remember this is an exercise in seeing, not in making lovely drawings. As your vision travels around the contours of your hand, you may need to connect certain contours with lines you don't see. It is all right to add these extra connecting lines to your drawing in order to keep your line continuous.

CONTOUR DRAWING

The eyes and hands are directed by the same mind. The hand knows what the eye knows. In the following exercises you will establish confidence in your hand/eye connection. The method is called contour drawing and was first explained by Kimon Nicolaides in his book, *The Natural Way To Draw*, published in 1941. It works because it helps students to use both sight and touch.

Contour drawing can be considered a starting point for all freehand drawing because it hooks up the hand and eye so the hand will draw what the eye sees. When concentrated, your eye and hand will work together recording your visual experience in detail.

Contour drawing is the first step to mastering freehand drawing. Once you have become comfortable with contour drawing, every other technique will be easy to add to your skill. Spend time learning contour drawing. Once you do, practice it often, forever! Do the exercises in this chapter as many times as necessary to be confident.

What Is A Contour?
When we look at a contour map we see lines that define levels of elevation. We also notice that there is a contour line where land and water meet. Think of a contour as the line that defines any edge.

In this chapter you will be drawing your hand—the hand that doesn't hold the pen. If you hold the pen in your right hand, then you will be drawing your left hand. Hold up your left hand. Notice the line where the skin meets the air. This is the outline or outside contour of your hand. Now rotate your hand. As you move it, notice the contour of skin meeting air changes.

Just as on a map, a contour is not only an exterior, but an interior line as well. Edges where *two different materials meet or where changes in plane occur* must be considered contour lines. Distinctive surface changes (hills and valleys) are also considered contours. If you are wearing jewelry these edges will be contours. Therefore, where skin meets air, fingernails, and jewelry there is a contour line. Any wrinkle or crease, changes in elevation—hills and valleys—of your hand will also be contour lines.

As you become aware of these lines, think of them as definition lines—lines that indicate a connection between two materials or two planes. For example, contours describe the connection between skin and air, land and water, vertical and horizontal.

In drawing we learn to consider the space around an object to be just as important as the object. This is a new way to look at the world. Most people see objects as separate and distinct. We learn to see everything in the world connected to something else, like a giant puzzle with all the pieces fitting together.

In the next series of exercises you are going to connect everything you see with one line. This line will be the record of your perception of your subject. The movement of your eye around the contours of any subject is continuous and unbroken. Your pen will record that movement.

Exploring and Discovering
As you begin practicing contour drawing, get the idea that you are exploring and discovering your subject *as if you are seeing it for the first time*. You can do this every time you draw, even with subjects you have drawn many times. Your experience will always be different and you will never get bored.

BLIND CONTOUR DRAWING

Blind contour drawing is a way of focusing your concentration as you draw. Of course it is not blind. Just the opposite. You are going to see very well indeed! It is called "blind" because you will not be seeing your drawing paper or the lines you are making. All attention is put on your drawing subject, whatever it is.

Blind contour drawing is the perfect warm-up when you sit down to draw. It puts you into a concentrated state of awareness. Because you cannot monitor what is happening on the paper, you can devote all your attention to observing your subject.

At first this may seem restricting, but as you practice you will find that it is liberating and relaxing. You must learn to trust yourself. The lines you are making are a perfect record of your perceptions.

Resist the temptation to look at your paper. Draw all the contours both inside and out. Don't be concerned whether your drawing is going to turn out looking like a hand. It may not. The important thing is you are learning to concentrate and see your subject in intimate detail. This is the way you must learn to see if you are going to draw experientially.

Get the idea that the point of your pen is actually touching your hand as you draw
Be careful to keep your pen point synchronized with your vision. Don't let your eyes get ahead or behind your pen point. You will be recording what you see at the moment of seeing. Keep the pen moving along at an even pace—whatever speed seems to be comfortable for you. Avoid stopping or hesitating. Keep your eye and pen moving for the entire drawing.

Ignore the internal dialogue that says "this is stupid," or "how can you expect to draw without looking at the paper?" Rather, focus your attention on the perceptual exploration and discovery that is taking place.

It is very important to do this exercise correctly, without looking at your paper until you have finished. When you are sure you have seen every contour you want to record, then it's time to take the pen off the paper and look at what you did. After this, and each subsequent drawing, write a sentence at the bottom of your sheet describing your experience.

Do this exercise as many times as necessary until you are confident you have established the hand-eye connection. Before you go on, be certain that you have learned what it feels like to concentrate and really see your subject.

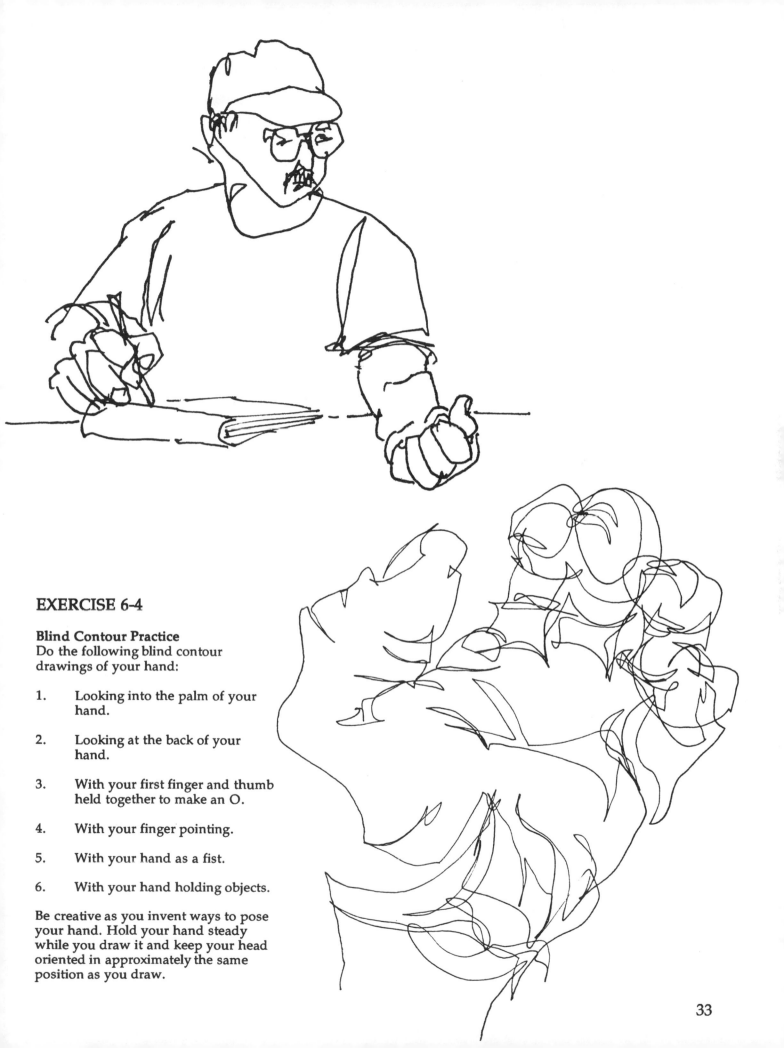

EXERCISE 6-4

Blind Contour Practice
Do the following blind contour drawings of your hand:

1. Looking into the palm of your hand.

2. Looking at the back of your hand.

3. With your first finger and thumb held together to make an O.

4. With your finger pointing.

5. With your hand as a fist.

6. With your hand holding objects.

Be creative as you invent ways to pose your hand. Hold your hand steady while you draw it and keep your head oriented in approximately the same position as you draw.

CHECK-BACK CONTOUR DRAWING

When you have mastered the blind contour technique, you are ready for the check-back contour drawing. The check-back is exactly like the blind contour except that you glance at the paper from time to time to check your proportions, angles, sizes, and so on. At first you may find that this glancing will interrupt your concentration. But with practice you will feel just as concentrated as when making the blind contour.

Blind contour drawing looking at the left hand in the mirror

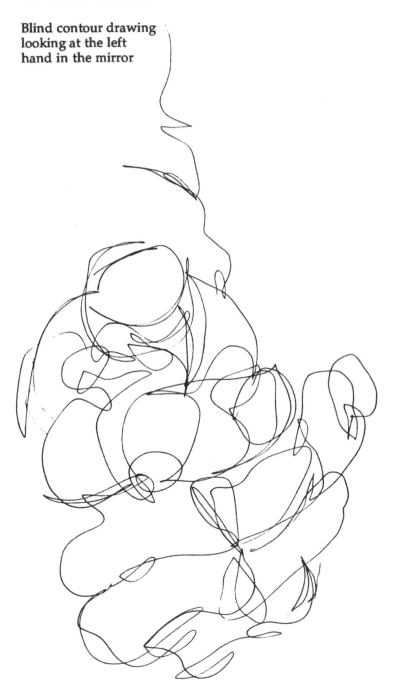

Check-Back Contour Drawing
This exercise is similar to the last, except that you are going to check your paper from time to time. Begin drawing as if you are doing a blind contour. When you feel you would like to check the paper, stop the movement of your pen and look at the paper. Then go back to your subject and continue your continuous-line contour.

With practice your checking will get faster. Eventually you'll be able to do it so fast that you need only slow the pen a bit. The glance to the drawing will take less than a second.

Each time you glance, notice what angle the lines you draw make to the horizontal or vertical. Notice the lengths of lines and how they relate to the ones you have already drawn. Note the position of each detail relative to what is already on the paper. Get interested in these relationships.

If you have not been accurate, do not be too concerned. Just notice the differences. Sometimes compensations can be made. Don't ever go over a line. Always make new lines. If you make a large error, just disregard it and make a new line where you think it should be.

As with the blind contour, keep the lines continuous. Examine each part of your hand as completely as possible before you go on to the next part. For example, draw your thumb and all the connections and wrinkles related to your thumb before continuing. Don't make one large outline of the hand and then fill in the details. That just doesn't work.

Glance only as often as you are compelled to. Five or ten times during one hand drawing should be plenty. There is no need to glance every second or two. That will interrupt your concentration. You should be drawing blind 95 percent of the time.

Be careful not to symbolize any portion of your subject. Everything you draw should be based only on what you see, not on what you *think* you see. For example, when you draw a wrinkle that occurs between two finger joints don't just make a back and forth line. Look carefully at the wrinkle and draw its contour as you see it.

As you do these continuous line drawings, remember that it will be necessary to put in some extra connecting lines—lines you don't see that help you get from one point to another without taking the pen off the paper.

Each time you finish drawing, remember to write a sentence at the bottom of your sheet describing what your experience was during that drawing exercise.

At first, some students find this exercise more difficult than the blind contour. They say they feel more responsible to have the proportions in the drawing accurate. Do not be too concerned if the proportions in your drawing are off. This is only normal. It usually takes many, many drawings before the proportions begin to make sense.

Accept the proportions as they occur. Often incorrect or exaggerated proportions are more exciting and fun to draw than the exact and perfect ones. So enjoy your strange proportions, have fun with them, and you will enjoy drawing more. Intentionally change or manipulate your proportions for emphasis. That is when the true artist in you begins to emerge.

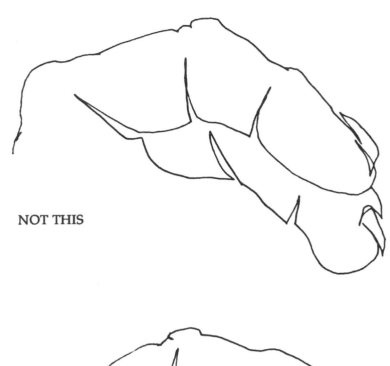

NOT THIS

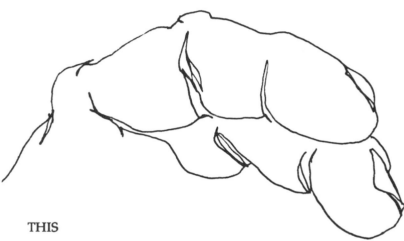

THIS

Carefully observed wrinkles and symbolically represented wrinkles

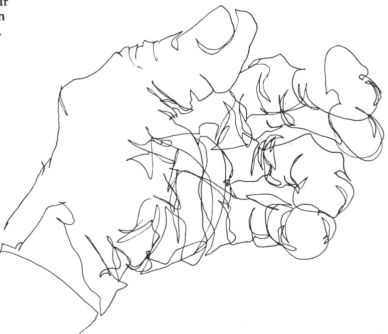

One-line blind contour drawing

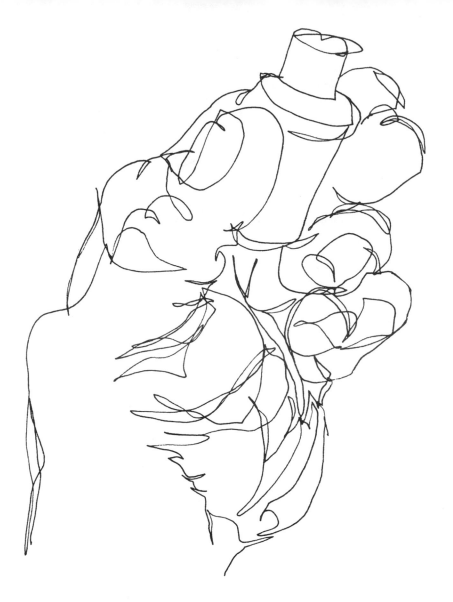

Check-back contour drawing

EXERCISE 6-6

Drawing With the Other Hand
Do a continuous-line check-back contour drawing holding the pen in your left hand if you are right-handed, or in your right hand if you are left-handed. Try posing the hand you are drawing in the hitch-hiker position for this drawing.

You may find that it feels easier or more comfortable drawing with the other hand. You may find that it feels awkward, but that you like the drawing more. Most people are pleasantly surprised the drawing comes out as well as it does. Don't underestimate your ability to draw with both hands. It is a fine idea to do it from time to time.

This exercise will help keep you conscious and aware of what you are doing—which is essential to drawing experientially. Remember to make some notes at the bottom of your sheet describing your experience.

EXERCISE 6-7

Hands Holding Objects
Take the time to establish your skill with contour drawing. Draw your hand holding various objects. Here are some suggestions: kitchen utensils, a coffee cup, vegetables, fruit, a pen, a flower, a glass, a spoon.

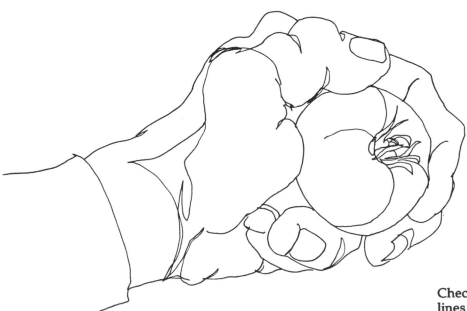

Check-back contour with interrupted lines

36

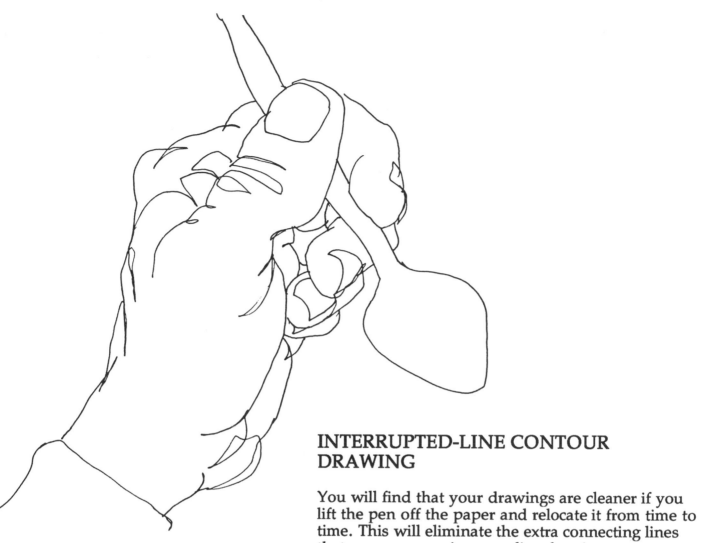

INTERRUPTED-LINE CONTOUR DRAWING

You will find that your drawings are cleaner if you lift the pen off the paper and relocate it from time to time. This will eliminate the extra connecting lines that are necessary in a one-line drawing.

This does not mean that you should draw with short, single lines. It is only a recommendation to simplify your drawing.

EXERCISE 6-8

Interrupted-Line Contour
Begin to eliminate extraneous lines by lifting the pen to relocate its position as you draw. Keep your lines as continuous as possible without adding lines that you don't see. Draw your hands holding various objects as you practice this.

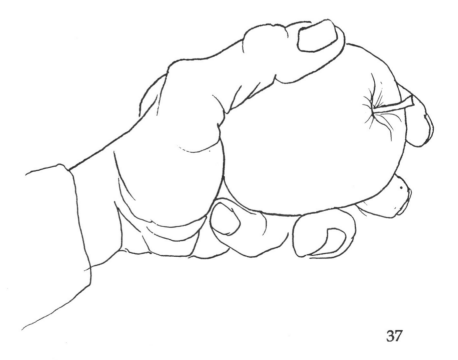

7

Making Distinctions

Drawing is a process of making distinctions. Any mark on the paper is a distinction. Lines define edges and contours of form, changes of plane, variations between materials, space in a drawing. Lines can also influence the feelings or emotional response of the person drawing or a viewer of a drawing.

LINES

There are delicate lines, bold lines, peaceful lines, vigorous lines, gentle lines, hard lines, living lines—the list can go on and on. Vertical lines can suggest energy, horizontal lines stability. Diagonal lines can imply movement or force. Curving lines can suggest softness, playfulness, even fun.

The most effective drawn line is the spontaneous line. It is a clean line, simply drawn, and appropriate to the moment—communicating the creative experience of the artist. A spontaneous line cannot be engineered to communicate. It just does.

As you draw, experiment with the line. Sometimes push on your pen, other times go easy. Move fast or slow. Use different drawing instruments—bamboo pens, steel-nib pens, bamboo sticks, brushes. You will find the possibilities are infinite. Select the drawing instrument that feels right to you and is appropriate for what you want to do.

EXERCISE 7-1

Line Experiments
Discover different ways you can make lines. See what you and your pen are capable of. Make 20 or more experiments. Draw light lines, dark lines, crisp lines, soft lines, curved lines, straight lines, angular lines, concave lines, convex lines, jagged lines, smooth lines—and more. Then look at each line and write down a specific emotion or feeling you can associate with it.

Wandering

Foolish

Moving

Wild

Confident

Floating

Decisive

Fast

Definitive

Soft

Energetic

Light

Dead

Dizzy

Troubled

Monotonous

Slow

Furry

Clarity

Beginners tend to make many light or tentative lines to define one edge. The edges of a subject drawn in this way will look hairy, messy, and indistinct. The technique is sometimes called "sketching it out". I call it "chicken scratching". These tentative, scratchy lines communicate hesitation and insecurity. If you have the habit of drawing this way, I recommend you practice contour drawing until you are able to be more decisive in your approach.

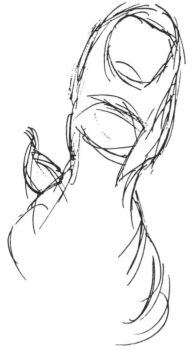

The "sketch it out" approach

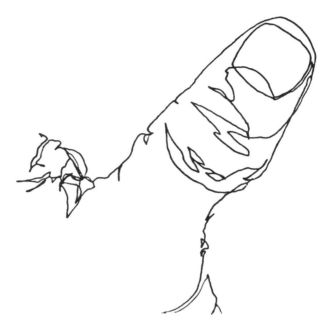

Slow continuous-line contour drawing

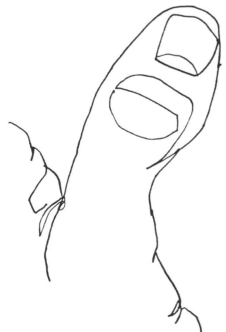

Quick continuous-line contour drawing

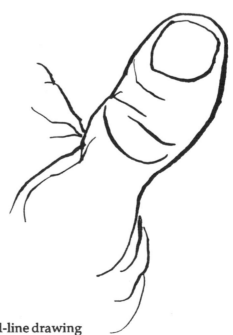

Interrupted-line drawing

SPACE AND FORM

Every line on a paper affects the total composition within the defined limits—the edges of the paper. The outside edge of an object is called its outline.

An outline separates the outer edges of an object from the space behind those edges. An outline defines a subject's form and also defines the space surrounding the subject. Space and form have the same line.

The space between the object and the edges of the paper is also a defined space. This space has form also.

Drawing of the negative space around a hand holding a fork

Negative space around a hand egg beater

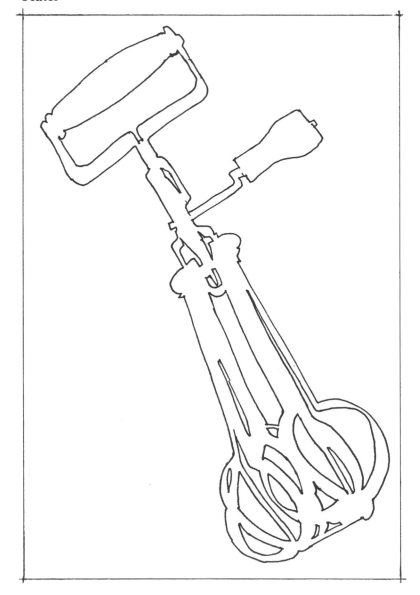

EXERCISE 7-2

Negative Space Awareness
Draw the negative space around your hand holding an object. Be careful not to draw your hand or the object. You are drawing only the common line between these figures and the space they occupy in your composition.

EXERCISE 7-3

Negative Space Awareness
Find a kitchen utensil or other object that has negative space within the form of the figure. A hand egg beater, a cheese slicer, a corkscrew, or a whisk are all excellent subjects to use for this exercise. Draw the negative spaces, without drawing the object. Indicate the space between the figure and the borders of the sheet as well as the space that is internal to the object. Increase the impact by darkening in the negative space as shown on Page 43. The easiest way to do this is to brush in non-waterproof black ink.

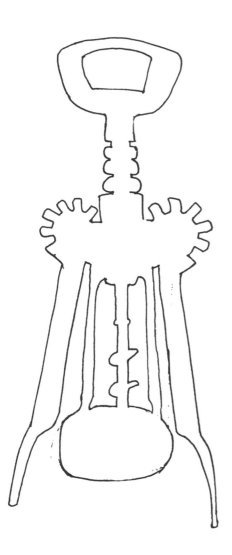

The black areas in this example represent the negative spaces.

Negative Space

In a drawing, the space outside an object is sometimes called negative space. It is also called the ground or background—as opposed to the figure—the object of attention. Negative space is also the space within the figure that is not part of the figure, such as the space between the spokes of a wheel. Negative space is essential to the composition and communication that occurs, though only the educated eye will look for it.

The shape of negative space is also determined by the format of the sheet. Most sketchbook paper is rectangular and can be used in a vertical or horizontal position. Each time you draw, consider a vertical or horizontal format before you begin. Select the one that will best accommodate your message. Your sheet format is, in effect, your frame. The way this frame interacts with your figure will affect the impact of your drawing.

This drawing was made by my four-year-old son on a long thin scrap of paper he found on my studio floor. 3" x 33 1/2", felt pen

COMPOSITION

I was amazed at the natural sense of composition my sons had between the ages of three and seven. Their drawings took advantage of the total sheet size and shape. Sometimes drawing on scraps of paper found on my studio floor, they would make striking compositions in line. I have found that most children have this natural ability until they go to school. Then they seem to lose it as they become concerned with being correct to avoid criticism. The ability to compose can be relearned by becoming aware of negative space and figure-ground relationships.

EXERCISE 7-4

Compositions
Make a number of unusual shaped pieces of paper by cutting up a sheet from your sketchbook. Now draw on them, taking advantage of the unusual shape of each sheet. Make your compositions extend to the perimeter of each sheet.

EXERCISE 7-5

Separate Straight Lines
Draw only straight lines on a page of your sketchbook. Let some of the lines touch the edges of the sheet, but don't let any line touch another line. Use lines of different lengths, and draw them at different angles. Don't make any parallel lines. When you've finished, look at the sheet and discover the spaces you have created.

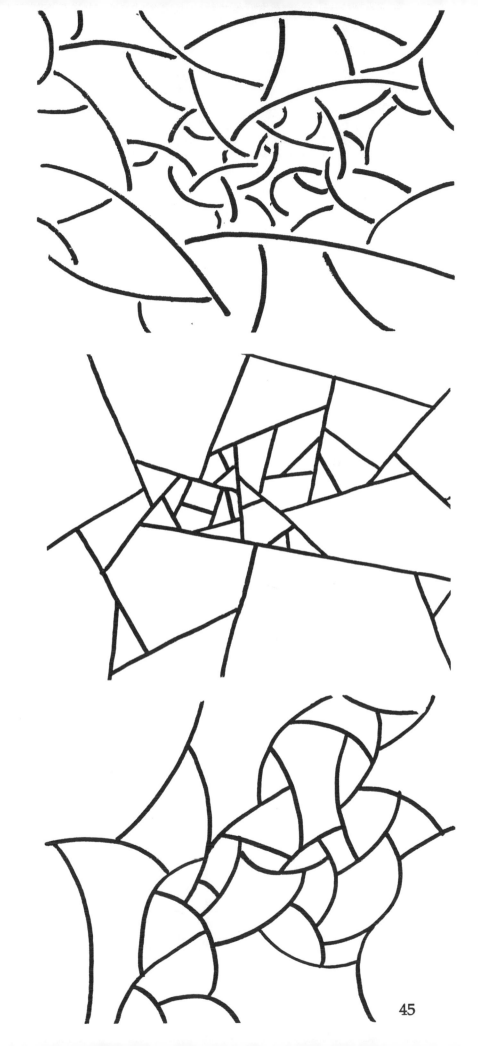

EXERCISE 7-6

Separate Curved Lines
Draw only curved lines on a page of
your sketchbook. Let some of the
curves touch the edge of the sheet.
Don't let any line touch another line.
Use only arches, not S curves. The
curves may arch in any direction you
please. When you've finished, look at
the sheet and notice the spaces you
have created.

EXERCISE 7-7

Connected Straight Lines
Draw straight lines on the paper at
random. Follow these rules. Each line
must touch at least one other line.
Never begin or end a line at the end of
another line. Never cross a line. Do not
draw any parallel lines. You may begin
drawing the lines from anywhere on
the sheet or from another line. When
the drawing is complete, all lines must
be touching other lines or the edge of
the sheet of paper.

When you've finished, look at the sheet
and notice the spaces you have created.
Notice which spaces appear to come
forward and which spaces appear to
recede.

EXERCISE 7-8

Connected Curved Lines
Draw only curved lines on the paper at
random. Follow these rules. Each line
must touch another line. Never begin or
end a line at the end of another line.
Never cross a line. Curve your lines
any way you wish, but use only arcs,
not S curves. Lines may begin from
space or from another line. When the
drawing is complete all lines must be
touching other lines or the edge of the
sheet of paper.

When you've finished, look at the sheet
and notice the spaces you have created.
Notice which spaces appear to come
forward and which spaces appear to
recede.

45

FIGURE AND GROUND

The figure is the object you focus on. The ground is everything around the figure. What is figure and what is ground can change, depending on your point of view. Take for example a desk in a room. The desk is a figure and the room is the ground. You notice a letter lying on the desk. Now the top of the desk is the ground and the letter is the figure. You wonder how the letter is addressed. Now the envelope is the ground and the address is the figure. You note that the stamp is foreign. Now the stamp is the figure, the envelope the ground. When you see the amount of the postage, the number on the stamp becomes the figure and the stamp itself the ground. Figure and ground perception depends upon your point of view.

This quick sketch was made on a river raft trip at Grand Teton National Park. The tall dead tree is the figure. Or is it the nest at the top of the tree? Or is it the osprey sitting in the nest? The answer depends on your point of view. 5 1/2" x 8 1/2", 1 minute

EXERCISE 7-9

Figure and Ground
In this exercise you will make a sheet with four compositions using black ink or cut-out pieces of black paper on white paper.

Divide the sheet into four quadrants by drawing a line down the middle and a line across the middle. In the first quadrant use only straight edges to outline a figure-ground composition in black and white. Let the white forms be figure. In the second, use only curved lines to outline a figure-ground composition with the black forms being figure. In the third, use both straight and curved lines. Arrange the composition so that both black and white figures occur. In the fourth, make an ambiguous composition using both straight and curved lines, where the figure-ground relationships in black and white can be reversed, depending on your point of view.

Four part figure and ground exercise

Full size detail from full figure life
drawing 22 1/2″ x 35″

48

8

Facing Faces

Beginning drawing students usually feel that drawing a face is an advanced proposition. They believe it needs a lot of practice and instruction. But Experiential Drawing does not require advanced theory or knowledge, only careful observation and awareness.

To face the facts of drawing faces, assume the attitude that drawing faces is like drawing anything. It can be attempted at any time. The real challenge comes in creating on paper a face drawn with personal expression that resembles the person. Since *trying* to create can end in frustration, I suggest that you put aside that goal for now. Instead, focus your attention on seeing your subject—the person's face—accurately. The rest will take care of itself.

The traditional approach suggests you study the proportions, features, skeletal structure, and muscles of the face before proceeding. Your approach will be to trust your experience, dive right in, and risk looking foolish. If you are a beginner, look at this as an adventure into the unknown. You will learn more quickly and you won't get lost in analysis and drudgery.

Seeing a Person's Face
In the American society, looking at people must be done with discretion. We are taught at an early age that it is not polite to stare at people. We become face-shy and don't really pay attention to the way people look.

But to draw a face you must give yourself permission to look carefully at a person's face—to see it in every detail. The experience of seeing and drawing a person's face can be one of the most profound you will ever have while drawing. To really see a person's face is to really see that person. If you have never tried it, prepare for an experience.

BLIND CONTOUR DRAWING

In the next exercise you are going to draw a person's face without looking at your paper. You should be well prepared for this drawing by now. You have practiced blind contour enough to understand the importance of being true to the exercise and not allowing even a glance at your paper. It will be particularly difficult with this exercise, however. You may have a very strong desire to see if the drawing is coming out the way you want it to.

The best way to prepare for this exercise is to acknowledge that your drawing will most likely have little resemblance to the person. It may not even look like a face. Agree before you start that you do not have to show what you have done to the person you are drawing. This way you will eliminate most disappointments. After all, a blind contour drawing can hardly be expected to actually look like the person.

Sometimes there are surprises. Even though the drawing is made blind and the features will most likely be out of alignment, there may be a resemblance to the person drawn. But don't get your hopes up. Just do the exercise and see what happens.

As you draw, refrain from naming the features you are drawing. Just observe. Forget about eyes, nose, and mouth. Treat the features of your subject as you would a hand or any other object. This is to avoid falling back on your learned symbolic representations. As you draw the contours, imagine that the point of your pen is actually touching each detail of the person's face.

EXERCISE 8-1

Blind Contour Drawing of a Face
With your roller-ball or fountain pen, face your subject and make a blind contour. It is a good idea to have your subject drawing you at the same time. That way you can check each other to be sure you don't look down at your drawings.

You can begin anywhere. For this exercise, begin with the top of the head and work down. Draw the hair by following along its contours. Notice the way it moves, waves, curls, and falls over the head in different directions. Notice where it sticks up and out. See where it lies down and back. It is obviously not necessary to draw every hair, but do take the time to establish, with line, enough of the movement so you will capture its essence.

Now move your line down to the eyes. Look at each eye and draw what you see. Don't fall into the trap of drawing a symbol for an eye. Look at that unique eye. Draw the eyebrow, the lid, the lashes, the folds of the eye. Draw the iris, the pupil, the corners of the eye, and the lower lid. Take your time and observe every detail. Then move your line to the other eye with the same attention.

Bring your line down and trace the outline around the nose. The mouth will need a line along the top of the upper lip, a line where the upper lip and the lower lip come together, and a line on the bottom of the lower lip. If the mouth is open and you can see teeth, draw them.

Trace around the chin. Draw the outline of the cheeks and the ears if you can see them. Be sure and include some of the neck and shoulders or your drawing will look like a face mask.

Remember that your drawing will include extra lines that you don't actually see, since your drawing is to be done with one continuous line.

When you are sure you have traced every single feature carefully, take the pen off the paper and look at what you have done. If you are like most students, you will probably have gone a bit too fast and you will see that you have missed something. You will also see that the face looks distorted and out of proportion. That is to be expected.

Now do the exercise again. Try it with the same person—or, if you feel you have done a complete job the first time, work with a new partner. Again, do it as a blind contour following the directions carefully.

DISTANCE AND PROPORTION

Most people have a pretty good eye when it comes to measuring distance and proportion. We began training our eyes when we were tiny babies reaching for food, rattles, and Mommy's nose. We use our ability to estimate distance every day to navigate our bodies through doorways and up and down stairs; to reach for food, papers, and writing utensils; to write, shake hands, and drive and park our bicycles and cars. All of these everyday activities take a trained eye. And we have learned these moves experientially. So, in pursuing drawing, be prepared to learn the same way.

Before proceeding with the next exercise, look at the proportions of a face to prepare for a more accurate drawing experience. Many beginners tend to draw the eyes up near the top of the head. This is because the eyes are closer to the hairline on the forehead than to the bottom of the chin. But the hairline is not the top of the head. The eyes are really about halfway between the top of the hair to the bottom of the chin. Each face is different, however. Some people don't even have hair. Others have a long face and a deep chin. So look at the face you are drawing before you start, and observe it carefully.

If you are drawing a good friend, ask for permission to touch his/her face. Actually put your hands on the face and feel where things are as you look with your eyes. This can be a great help to experiencing and understanding the person's face.

The bottom of the nose is usually about midway between the eyes and the chin. The mouth is located about one-third the distance below the bottom of the nose and chin. That is, if you are looking at an average face straight on—but most faces are not average and your view is seldom straight on. Always draw from your actual experience of seeing.

If drawing in proportion is desired, you must learn to do careful observation and measurement. If not, have fun and accept your exaggerated and out-of-proportion expressions.

EXERCISE 8-2

Check-Back Contour Drawing of a Face

Make a continuous-line, check-back drawing of a face with your roller-ball pen or your fountain pen. Proceed as outlined in the last exercise, but check your progress as you draw to be sure you are drawing the features where you want them.

Be careful that you don't get too involved in what is happening on the paper. Take your time and keep your attention on your subject. Stay in tune with your experience.

The entire drawing is done with one continuous line. Remember that it is permissible to put in as many extra lines as necessary. Draw as large as your paper will permit and do not retrace any lines you draw.

Quick one-line profile contour

EXERCISE 8-3

Profile—Continuous-Line Blind Contour
Make a blind contour drawing of your subject in profile. Be particularly careful with the face line described above. Keep your drawing large on the sheet. Be sure to include the back of the head, the neck, and some of the shoulders.

Profile
The key line in a profile drawing is the line that begins with the hair and comes down the forehead, defines the nose and mouth, outlines the chin, and continues down the neck.

Viewed in profile, the distance from the bottom of the chin to the bridge of the nose is about the same as from the bridge of the nose to the back of the ear.

The distance from the top of the head to the chin is about the same as from the bridge of the nose to the back of the head.

Typical measurement errors are bringing the ear too far forward or making the head too narrow. Remember that the eyes are located about half way between the top of the head and the chin.

If you are working with other students, arrange yourselves so that each of you presents his or her profile to another student. A good way to do this is to put four persons at a table, two facing into the table, and two turning their chairs 90 degrees.

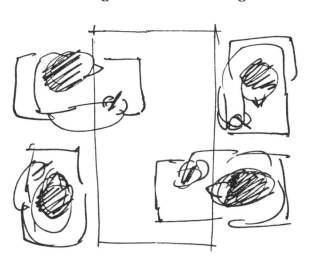

Check-back contour

USING DIFFERENT MEDIA

In the next series of exercises you will try out different media and get more comfortable and experienced at drawing people's faces.

Don't be nervous. Take advantage of the opportunity to explore and experience people in this intimate way. Put your whole self into these drawings, let go of your inhibitions, and express yourself drawing.

Refrain from judging your drawing. If ink spills or smears or drips onto your drawing, accept that as part of the project. Just let it happen and continue drawing. Have fun and discover what a pleasure drawing can be.

EXERCISE 8-4

Profile—Check-Back Contour
With your roller-ball pen or fountain pen, make a number of check-back contour drawings with only one line. Then do some with an interrupted line. Take your time and observe carefully. Draw what you see, not what you think you see.

EXERCISE 8-5

Bamboo Stick Check-Back Drawing
Draw a face with your bamboo stick,
using the check-back method. Relocate
your lines as often as you feel
necessary. Keep the drawing large on
the sheet. Dip the stick into your bottle
of ink and tap it a few times on the
edge of the bottle to let the extra ink
drip back into the container. Draw with
the stick until it is out of ink. It is not
necessary that the ink flow be full-
strength or uniform. Be careful not to
scratch over lines to make them darker.
Let the dry gray lines also be part of the
drawing to make a dynamic variation in
line weight and tone. If you feel like
making variations and exaggerations as
you draw, go ahead. Use lines that
have a continuous flow as you work
with the contours.

EXERCISE 8-6

Bamboo Pen Check-back Drawing
Draw your subject's face with the
bamboo pen, using the check-back
method. See your drawing on the sheet
in your mind's eye before you begin.
Do a quick drawing of the face in the
air over the sheet before you make any
marks on the paper.

Follow the same instructions given in
the last exercise. The pen will give you
a bit more control than the stick. Pay
particular attention to detail—hair, eyes,
mouth. Watch your proportions only if
they are important to you.

Bamboo stick check-back drawing

Bamboo pen check-back drawing using
interrupted lines

55

Contour caricature drawing

CARICATURE

A caricature is a drawing made with ludicrous exaggeration. Artists have made a very good living doing caricatures of political figures and celebrities.

Caricature artists analyze the face and pick out the features that are characteristic of the personality. They usually work from photographs and will make a number of trials before the final drawing is completed. Mouths and expressions are enlarged; other features are exaggerated larger or smaller until the overall effect is entertainingly and unmistakably the known personality. It is not an easy trick and requires practice and experience.

The typical street caricature artist does a profile to a learned formula and often will apply a small body engaging in some activity the person enjoys. These drawings are done fast. Some really look like the person, but most need a good deal of imagination to see a likeness.

EXERCISE 8-7

Caricature Drawing
This is definitely not an exercise to be concerned about. Do it in fun. Draw your subject's face with exaggeration. Typically noses are made larger. The eyes are put higher on the head unless the person has a high forehead. The chin is made into a feature, facial hair grows longer and bushier, the mouth is larger, the neck and upper body are small.

The rule here is to take prominent features and enlarge or diminish them in size. This is a great exercise for many students to discover that it won't hurt to put a bit more exaggeration into their serious drawings.

Use the pen or bamboo stick and draw with clean contour lines, exaggerating the features. Enjoy yourself.

56

EXERCISE 8-8

Self-Portrait
Set up a mirror and draw your self-portrait. A small pocket mirror will work fine. Use the bamboo pen, stick, a roller-ball, or fountain pen. Don't be too critical if it doesn't look like you. You might surprise yourself. Be sure and make a record of your experience at the bottom of the sheet.

If you prop up your mirror on your table surface, it will give you a view of your face looking up from the table top—a view that you don't usually have of yourself.

EXERCISE 8-9

Self-Caricature
Draw a continuous-line caricature of yourself with your pen. Exaggerate your features as much as you like. This is an excellent drawing to help you take yourself less seriously. If you have large ears, make them bigger. If you have a small nose, make it smaller. If you have a lot of hair, give yourself more. Do this exercise as many times as necessary until you get a drawing you like.

Self-portrait with a bamboo stick

Self-caricature

SELF-PORTRAIT

Self-portraits are a great way to practice observing a face in the frontal viewing position. But, more than that they can be involving and deeply personal experiences. We look at our faces in the mirror every day. But when you draw your own face experientially, you will see yourself in a new way. Some people may feel uneasy doing this at first, but this is normal. But if you get into the process of looking carefully and drawing, you will soon find yourself caught up in discovering your subject—you.

57

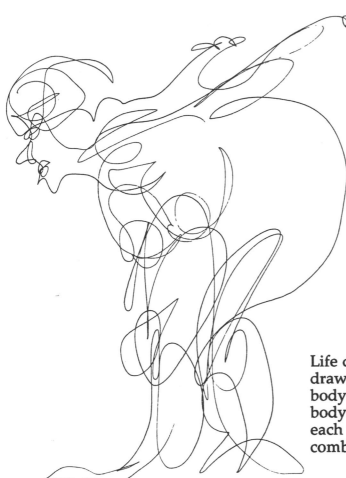

Energetic blind contour
17" x 14", 1 minute

EXERCISE 9-1

Blind Contour Warm-up
Blind contour drawings are a perfect
warm-up. Make a series of one to three-
minute blind contour drawings with
your roller-ball pen or fountain pen.
(Reread the section on contour drawing
in Chapter 6 before you begin.) The
purpose of these drawings is to connect
with the model—to observe the figure
carefully and establish your eye-hand
connection. All of the following
exercises should be done on 18" x 24"
paper, or larger.

9

Life Drawing

Life drawing is the ultimate opportunity to hone
drawing skill. Of all the subjects to draw, the human
body will challenge you forever. Not only is each
body different, but each pose taken by a model and
each viewing point is also different. The
combinations are infinite.

MODEL SESSIONS

Most life drawing will occur in a classroom
situation—either with a teacher or in an open model
studio where you pay a small fee and draw a model
for two to six hours. Check with the art department
of your local college or university to find out when
and where these sessions are scheduled.

If you are a beginner, refrain from comparing what
you are doing with what the other people in the
room are doing. Be there for yourself. Know that
you have a mission of your own—that you are there
to draw. Be enthusiastic, be serious, and
concentrate.

Have respect and appreciation for the model, who is
a working professional. Although modeling for
artists may look easy, it is not. I recommend that
every student try posing, clothed or nude, for 10 or
20 minutes. That way you can really appreciate what
is required to hold a position steady on the model's
platform. It is difficult. Our bodies want to move
constantly!

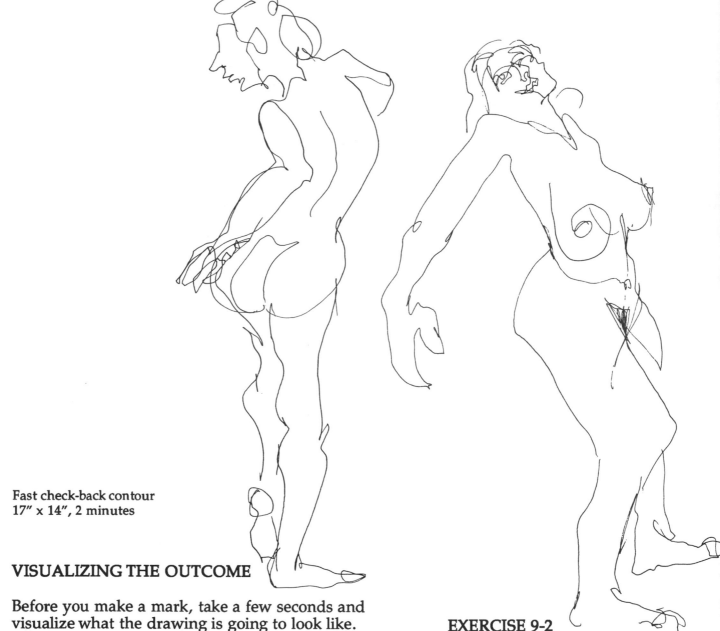

Fast check-back contour
17" x 14", 2 minutes

VISUALIZING THE OUTCOME

Before you make a mark, take a few seconds and visualize what the drawing is going to look like. Visualize the composition, the placement of the subjects on the page, the sizes and shapes, the space and forms. This can be done in a matter of seconds. Move your pen over the paper without touching it, pretending to draw. You will be amazed at how much easier it will be to accomplish your task when you do this. Then when you draw, it feels like you have already done it.

Maintain your attitude of exploration and discovery. Explore with your eyes and your drawing hand. Realize that most of what you do, at least in the beginning, will probably end up in the waste basket. Don't be too concerned about the results. Enjoy the experience.

If you put yourself into the creative process and get emotionally involved, life drawing can be very energizing.

EXERCISE 9-2

Continuous-line Check-back Contour Drawings
Do a number of check-back contour drawings with the steel-tipped dip pen or the calligraphy pen. Make continuous lines, but relocate your pen each time you dip or whenever you feel it is necessary to eliminate extra connecting lines. There is no need to put in any extra lines in this exercise unless you feel they are needed to maintain your concentration.

Work to the edges of your sheet. Work with the full figure but plan it so that the forms connect with at least three sides of the sheet. This will automatically improve your chances for balanced figure/ground compositions. Four- to six-minute poses should be adequate.

60

EXERCISE 9-3

**Interrupted-Line Contours—Bamboo
Pen and Stick**
For these exercises, draw separate
contour lines. It is not necessary to
make them continuous or add extra
lines. Draw the forms, musculature,
connections, and perspective by letting
your lines describe and even exaggerate
the most subtle variations.

This exercise requires careful
observation. Give yourself enough time
for these drawings. Eight- to ten-minute
poses should be adequate. If you use
more, you may begin to slow down and
get critical. A faster pace requires more
speed and less thought.

EXERCISE 9-4

Ovals
This is an excellent exercise for feeling
the form. Begin your drawing by
simplifying the model, using a series of
thin-line ovals all connected to describe
the basic form. Do these thinner lines
quickly with your roller-ball pen. Then
attack the drawing with the stronger
ink lines of the bamboo pen or stick,
and draw the actual contours over the
predrawn ovals. Six to ten minutes is
plenty for these drawings.

Fast expressive drawing with the
bamboo stick 23" x 35", 3 minutes

EXERCISE 9-5

Fast Drawing with the Bamboo Stick
Using the full sheet, really let go and
draw fast. Draw exaggerated, playful
forms. Leave out parts. Emphasize the
head, hands, and feet. These drawings
are caricature-like, drawn with a lot of
energy and abandon. Three- to four-
minute poses are long enough.

EXERCISE 9-6

Pen Drawings
Use a calligraphy pen, dip pen, or
fountain pen to draw your model in
detailed line. Do not lay out these
drawings with pencil first. Always work
directly from the form. Let your lines be
spontaneous. Connect your lines to at
least three edges of the sheet even if
you want to include background or the
suggestion of background. Limit the
drawing time of each pose to ten
minutes or less. Do this exercise often
with both male and female models.

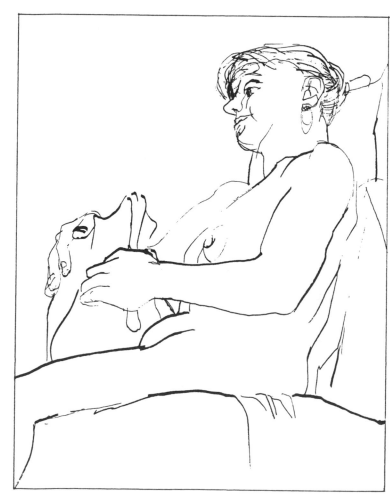

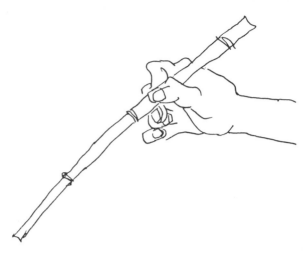

Hold the stick at least half way back

EXERCISE 9-7

The Foreshortened Figure
With the bamboo pen or stick, draw single-line contours to describe the figure in particularly foreshortened postures. Trust your eyes. Draw what you see, not what you think you see. Limit each pose to ten minutes or less.

FORESHORTENING

By shortening some of the lines in a drawing, you can give the illusion of forms actually coming forward or going back from the two-dimensional surface of the picture plane. This process, known as foreshortening, really is a simple one, but many people find it difficult. Almost every pose will give some opportunities for foreshortening.

When confronted with an arm or leg or whole body that must be drawn foreshortened, all you need to do is maintain one point of view and just draw exactly what you see.

Beginners are not always willing to trust this method, they may try to figure out how to draw the foreshortened subject so it looks right. Because this approach is based more on what a person knows or tries to figure out than on what he or she sees, it usually fails. This is not drawing from experience but from reason, taking one below the imaginary magic line mentioned in Chapter 1.

The foreshortened figure with the bamboo stick 18" x 24", 7 minutes

If you ask, "How do I draw that leg so it looks like it's coming toward me?," the answer is, "you don't need to know how." Just *trust your vision and draw what you see.*

Learned principles of foreshortening and perspective are only to help us to understand our seeing. Remember, any time you question how to draw something, all you need to know is right in front of your eyes. What you see will always be the correct answer. Trust your eyes and the ability of your hand to record what your eyes see.

EXERCISE 9-8

The Foreshortened Figure
Using the calligraphy pen, do a series of drawings of the foreshortened figure. Be particularly careful to record detail, facial features, fingers, toes, finger, and toe nails. The calligraphy pen will give you the opportunity to make thick and thin lines. Use them to modulate your expression of the model. Limit each pose to 12 minutes or less.

EXERCISE 9-9

Exaggerated Foreshortening
Using your calligraphy pen, make single-line contour drawings of the model in foreshortened poses. Intentionally exaggerate the perspective, making the parts of the anatomy that come toward you particularly large and the parts that are farthest away smaller. Use the thick and thin line possibilities of the calligraphy pen to accentuate this perspective. Limit each pose to 12 minutes or less.

Calligraphy pen drawings of foreshortened figures, each 17" x 23", 10 minutes

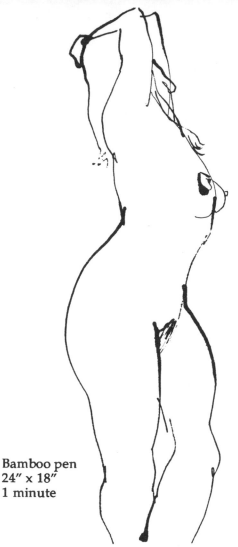

Bamboo pen
24" x 18"
1 minute

EXERCISE 9-10

Countdown

The purpose of this exercise is to free you up and get you drawing without thinking. This is a great sequence to use whenever a life-drawing session gets bogged down and the attitudes become too critical.

Using the bamboo stick, begin with an eight-minute pose. Then reduce the time for each drawing after that by one minute. Continue to work on capturing the entire figure each time. Keep your eyes on the model and work fast.

When you finish the one-minute pose, do a 45-second pose, a 30-second pose, and a 15-second pose. The shorter times will give your model opportunities to assume wonderfully creative and athletic poses. If it feels more comfortable, change to your roller-ball or fountain pen for the faster poses.

Remember to make a note about your experience when you have finished the series.

CAPTURING THE ESSENCE

Every artist wants to capture the essence of his or her subject. Experiential Drawing methods will get you closer to the essence than any other method. You will not achieve essence by trying for it—it will be apparent when you draw with honesty and integrity.

Instead of trying to make a good drawing, observe with all your senses and be true to your experience. On occasion you will come up with a drawing that will be pure essence. How can you recognize essence? It is just something that you will feel—that you will know intuitively.

Working Fast

I tell my students, "Don't hurry, but don't dawdle either." Sometimes it is a great idea to intentionally work faster or slower than you ordinarily work. Intentionally working fast can produce energetic, free-flowing results. It will always help in loosening a tight self-conscious drawing habit. Do it often.

Calligraphy pen
17" x 23", 2 minutes

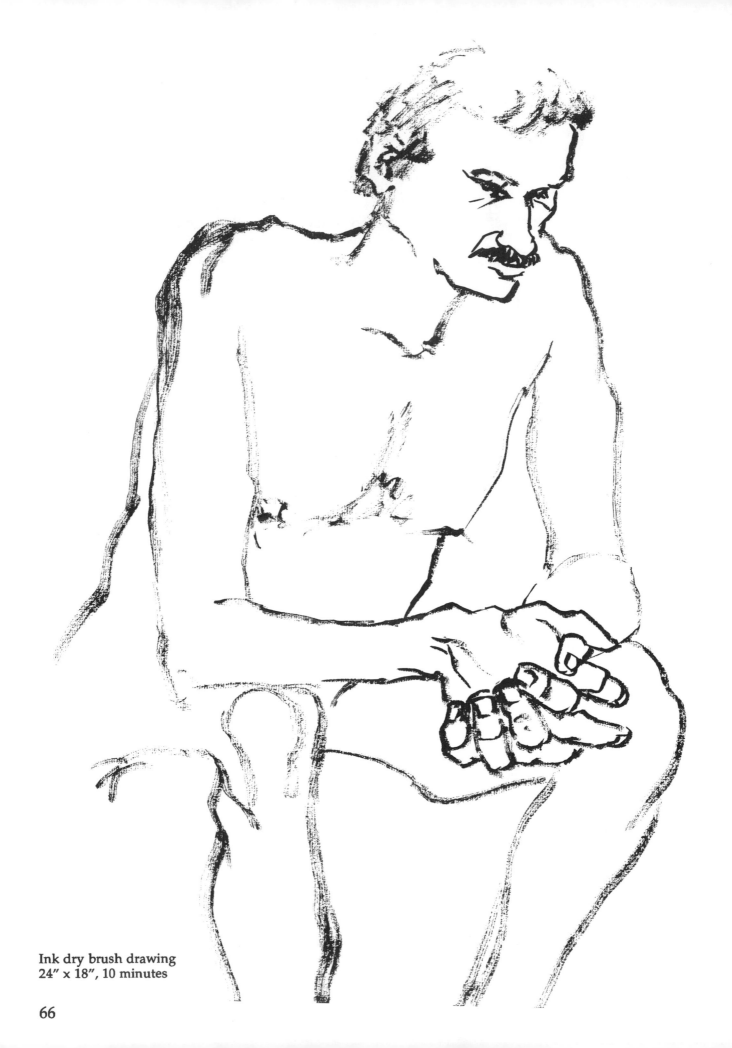

Ink dry brush drawing
24" x 18", 10 minutes

EXERCISE 9-11

Hands
Develop at least ten detailed drawings of hands performing different activities. Make three drawings with your calligraphy pen, three with the bamboo pen, and three with the bamboo stick. Draw two hands holding a pair of glasses, a piece of fruit, some flowers, a tennis racket. Observe each joint, draw the creases, bulges, and fingernails. Practice drawing hands until you love to draw them!

EXERCISE 9-12

Feet
Do at least ten studies of feet in different positions. Draw them from the bottom, from the top, crossed, walking, touching each other. You can draw your own feet by putting a mirror on the floor.

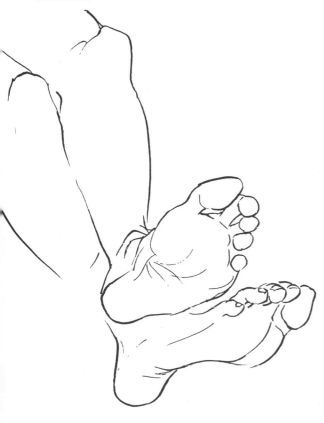

THE FACE AND THE FIGURE

When drawing a model, pay particular attention to the head and face. A well-drawn face will help you as you work on the rest of the figure. It can be discouraging to work on drawing a figure when the face has been carelessly observed and drawn. Always spend a little extra time to see and draw facial expression. It will help you maintain your enthusiasm for the rest of the pose. Never leave the face blank, even as a beginner.

Calligraphy pen drawing of hands
24" x 18", 10 minutes

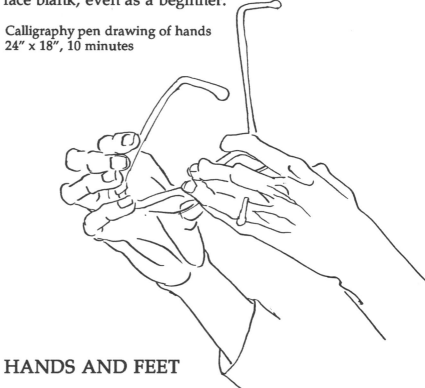

HANDS AND FEET

Hands and feet can inspire—their position communicates. Often we talk with our hands. Dancers gesture with both hands and feet.

Drawing the human figure requires special attention to the hands and feet. Beginning drawing students tend to disregard the hands and feet, or try and draw them without studying them. But they are extremely important. Since the hands and feet of a figure are so expressive, to draw them requires careful attention to each detail. Take time to observe hands and feet carefully. It is well worth the effort.

Beginners often draw hands and feet too small. If you are having that problem, become aware of it, and consciously make them larger than you think they need to be. Look at the wonderful large hands and feet on Rodin's sculptures for inspiration. In life drawing, well-drawn hands and feet are as important as a well-drawn face.

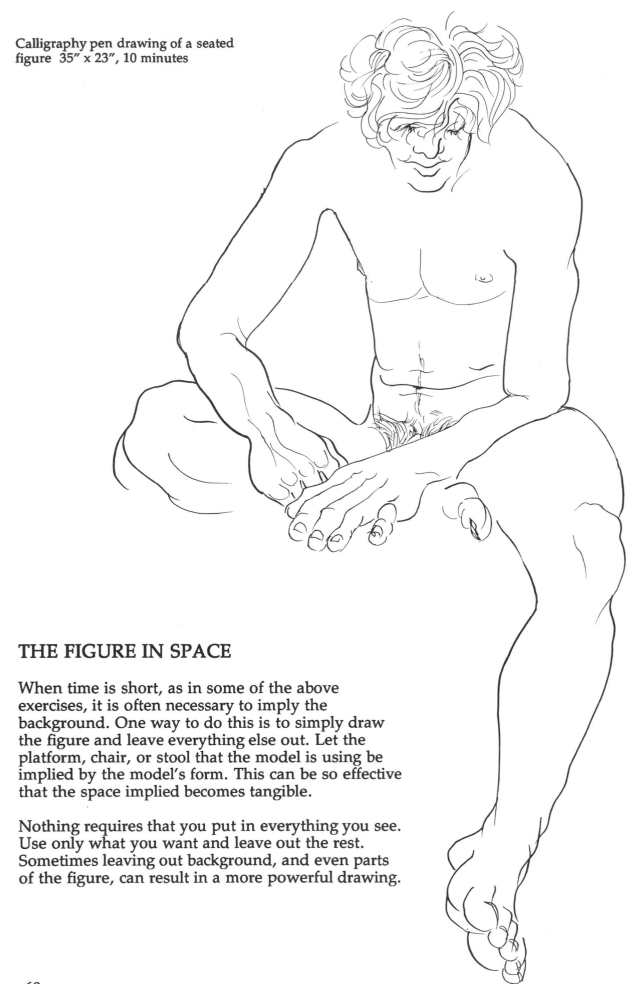

Calligraphy pen drawing of a seated
figure 35" x 23", 10 minutes

THE FIGURE IN SPACE

When time is short, as in some of the above
exercises, it is often necessary to imply the
background. One way to do this is to simply draw
the figure and leave everything else out. Let the
platform, chair, or stool that the model is using be
implied by the model's form. This can be so effective
that the space implied becomes tangible.

Nothing requires that you put in everything you see.
Use only what you want and leave out the rest.
Sometimes leaving out background, and even parts
of the figure, can result in a more powerful drawing.

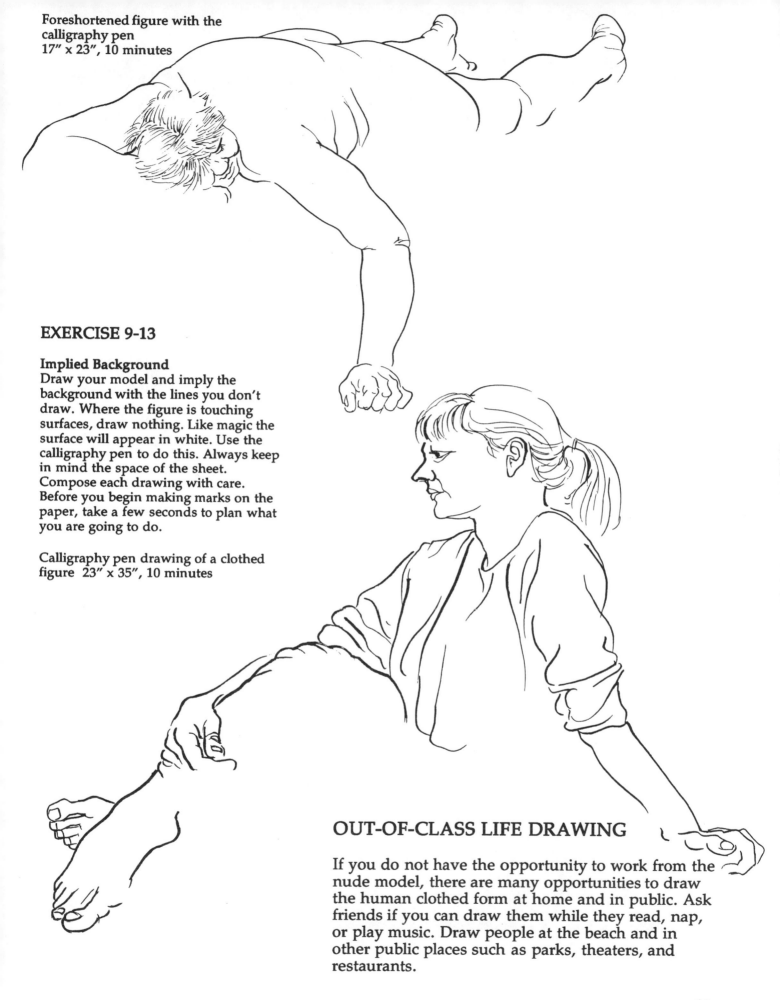

Foreshortened figure with the
calligraphy pen
17" x 23", 10 minutes

EXERCISE 9-13

Implied Background
Draw your model and imply the
background with the lines you don't
draw. Where the figure is touching
surfaces, draw nothing. Like magic the
surface will appear in white. Use the
calligraphy pen to do this. Always keep
in mind the space of the sheet.
Compose each drawing with care.
Before you begin making marks on the
paper, take a few seconds to plan what
you are going to do.

Calligraphy pen drawing of a clothed
figure 23" x 35", 10 minutes

OUT-OF-CLASS LIFE DRAWING

If you do not have the opportunity to work from the
nude model, there are many opportunities to draw
the human clothed form at home and in public. Ask
friends if you can draw them while they read, nap,
or play music. Draw people at the beach and in
other public places such as parks, theaters, and
restaurants.

Lifetree
Pencil drawing
25" x 36"   100 hours

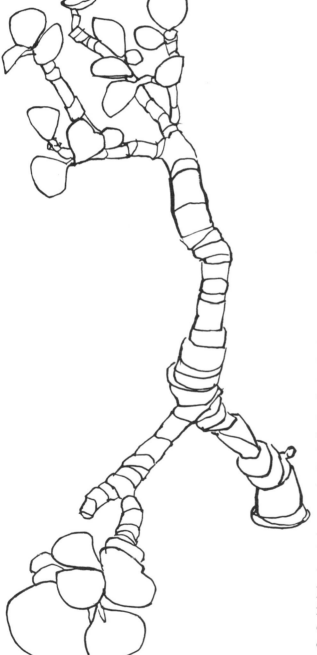

10

Creating Illusions

The experience of freehand drawing is a personal voyage. You have been engaging in this exploration for your own purposes. The products of your journey—your drawings—can be shared with others. There are technical skills that can enhance their message. But remember that techniques are not the secret to drawing, nor are they even needed to enjoy and appreciate it.

The best techniques are those you invent yourself. They become your signature—your style. Many techniques come out of personal inquiry, "What would be an effective way to describe that texture; capture the moment; improve the composition; distinguish the light, shade, and shadow; enhance the three-dimensional quality of this subject?" Others can be learned—the tricks artists use to fool the eye.

LINES

Up to now you have been working with the contour line. You have used a number of different drawing instruments providing a variety of lines—thin, thick, dark, and light. You have also seen that working fast or slow and with different degrees of energy can give you different kinds of lines. Many artists have become known for their line quality.

Vincent Van Gogh is known for his intense, passionate, impulsive lines. He used a variety of swirling strokes, short strokes, and even dots and dashes in his drawings. He loved the reed pen with its chisel point, similar to what we call the bamboo pen in this book.

Vincent Van Gogh, *Cypresses and Stars*

Rembrandt van Rijn made brush line drawings with energy and vitality similar to that found in Japanese Sumi and Chinese brush drawings. He drew with spontaneity using a variety of strokes—short and long, thick and thin, free and controlled.

Rembrandt van Rijn, *Christ Washing the Disciples' Feet*

The Zen artist uses an "enlightened" brush stroke—the living brush stroke that communicates life. It is the essence of energy. The combinations of these succinct strokes and their spatial relationships produce an animated quality of drawing.

Tatsuo Saito, *Squirl on a Grape Vine*

Pablo Picasso draws with expressive good humored lines. He plays with proportions and textures. Picasso draws clean contour lines which contrast with shorter more decorative lines.

Pablo Picasso, *23-6-68 I*

Albrecht Durer, perspective demonstration

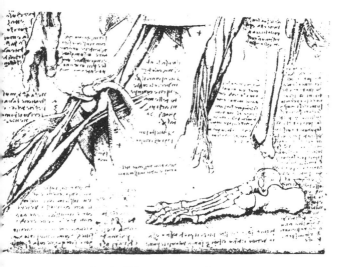

Leonardo da Vinci, scientific detail

Slow carefully drawn line

Clean quickly drawn line

Albrecht Durer's hand is disciplined, controlled, and intellectual.

Leonardo da Vinci drew with a quill ink line that was loose and free; but visually descriptive and incisive. He applied hatching and cross-hatching to define his subjects with care.

In the same way, your drawing signature will show a line quality that is characteristic of you. Look at your drawings and notice what you like about your line quality. Begin to develop your own unique style as you draw. Remember, no one will draw the way you do. Don't try to draw like others. Find your own way.

Let each line you make have an integrity of its own. Get in the habit of leaving your lines alone—never retracing them. If you draw over a line you have already made, you destroy the integrity of that line. When two lines rather than one define a contour, the eyes become confused. They don't know which line to recognize as the true line. To avoid this kind of ambiguity in a drawing, leave the lines you make alone.

If you want a dark line, make it dark to begin with. Keep your lines distinct, deliberate, and definite—the three D's of drawing. If you practice contour drawing, you will never again feel compelled to use the sketchy, chicken-scratched line—an indecisive approach to drawing.

Curving lines and moving lines are more decorative and lyrical. Straight lines are more static and structural.

The way you put lines together is important. Corners can be closed, open, overlapped, well defined, or ambiguous.

Basically, all lines drawn freehand fall into two categories. Neither is better or worse than the other.

Example 1: A line made slowly and deliberately. You can see small variations due to the minute movements of the nervous system. This line can be delicate, vibrant, and intimate.

Example 2: A line made quickly which can be clean, strong, powerful and energetic.

THE ILLUSION OF DEPTH

There are several ways to strengthen the basic contour line drawing to fool the eye into seeing three dimensions on a two-dimensional surface. The paper is flat, most objects we draw are not. But what we perceive we believe. Perception is a learned skill. When we see we use learned perceptual cues. When we draw we can employ these same learned cues to create convincing illusions.

Variation in the thickness of lines enhances the illusion of depth. Heavier lines indicate main outlines or a closer position. Lighter and thinner lines indicate more distant objects or less important contours. We emphasize with thicker and darker lines.

OVERLAPPING

Overlapping means putting one object in front of another. Most drawings of objects employ some overlapping. If you go back and look at your drawings of hands, you will see that you drew fingers in front of other fingers. By drawing what you see and not drawing what you don't see, you automatically produce the illusion of depth through overlapping.

Figure 1 shows three rectangles—a simple two dimensional diagram. In Figure 2, a line has been added. Now the three rectangles appear to be covering the line. Your eye tells you the line continues under each rectangle, even though it does not. In Figure 3, the illusion is three rectangles covering a fourth, long rectangle.

Simpler subjects tend to dominate more complex subjects in a drawing. Figure 4 looks like one square overlapping the corner of another square. It is really a four-sided rectangle and a six-sided rectangle meeting. But we don't perceive it that way. We perceive the simpler shape dominating the more complex shape. In Figure 5, we perceive a square missing one corner, lying on top of another square. But this is really a six-sided figure and an eight-sided figure coming together. Again, the simplest figure, the six-sided one, will dominate the more complex one. If we put two six-sided figures together as in Figure 6, we have equal complexity and the resulting impression is ambiguous.

74

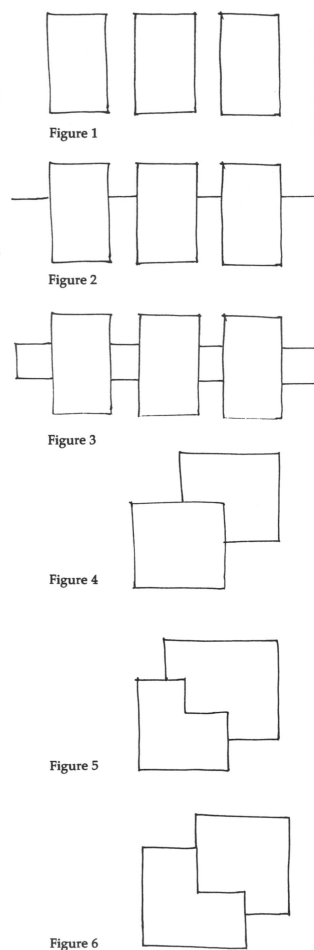

Figure 1

Figure 2

Figure 3

Figure 4

Figure 5

Figure 6

Figure 7

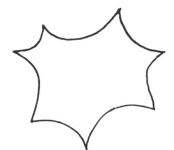

Figure 8

Figure 9

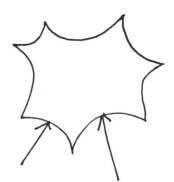

Figure 10

EXERCISE 10-1

Flower Overlap Drawing
Study and draw a real flower. Work on a large sheet of paper— 18" X 24" or 14" x 17".

Be particularly careful to employ overlapping. Draw what is closest to you first, then add what is immediately behind that, and so on.

Notice how the overlapping creates the illusion of depth.

CONCAVE AND CONVEX LINES

In Figure 7, we see a bulbous shape made up of convex lines. It appears as a solid form on top of the white ground of the paper. In Figure 8, we see a series of concave lines. The perceptual impression is an opening in the paper. The lines of forces between the figure and the ground in these two examples is diagramed in Figures 9 and 10.

The human body is solid and basically convex. An opening in the form, such as the space between the arm and chest, is usually concave. In a drawing, the solids and voids can be represented with concave and convex lines.

RELATIVE SIZE

Another way we perceive depth is in the relative size of the objects. A tree that is in the foreground will appear much larger than a tree that is in the background. Relative size can be a very powerful depth cue in a drawing.

Male figure showing concave and convex shapes
23" x 17", 10 minutes

EXERCISE 10-2

Close-up Fingers

Make a continuous-line contour
drawing of your hand with the fingers
coming toward you. Use your roller-ball
or fountain pen. This is a foreshortened
view, and for it to succeed you must
draw only what you see. Do it quickly
without thinking. Notice how large the
fingertips appear in relation to the
wrist.

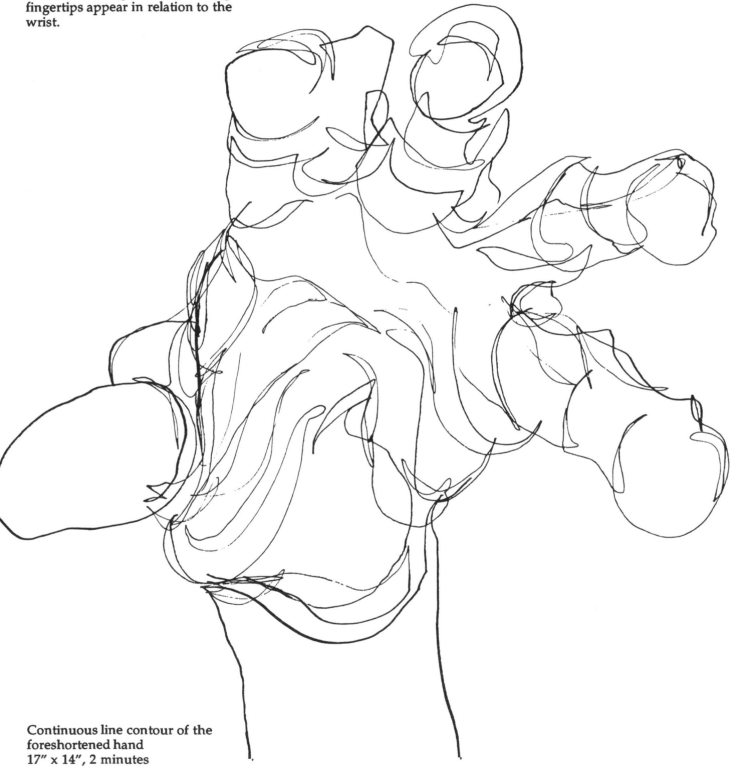

Continuous line contour of the
foreshortened hand
17" x 14", 2 minutes

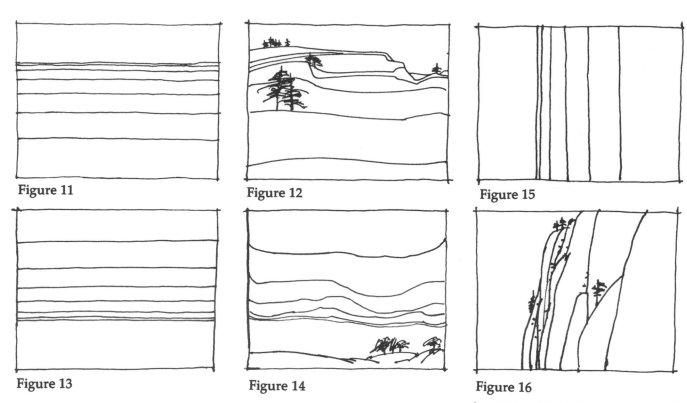

Figure 11

Figure 12

Figure 15

Figure 13

Figure 14

Figure 16

GRADIENTS

Gradients are another means that can be used to
emphasize depth. Figure 11 shows a linear density
gradient. With your imagination you can almost see
a flat plain, or a view of the ocean. Figure 12
demonstrates how the density gradient can be used
to create an illusion of depth in a landscape sketch.

In Figure 13, the density gradient is turned over.
Now it might remind us of cloud formations. Figure
14 shows the gradient used in a sketch of a cloud
formation.

Turning the density gradient on its side can indicate
a vertical barrier or cylindrical form, as in Figure 15.
In Figure 16, the vertical gradient is used to suggest
depth in a sketch of a cliff face.

A texture gradient is shown in Figure 17. In Figure
18, the texture gradient helps to indicate distance.

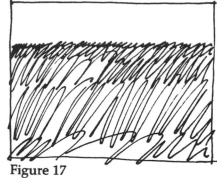

Figure 17

Figure 18

EXERCISE 10-3

In your sketchbook, use hatching to indicate shade and shadow as in Figure 19 or Figure 20. Hatching lines can be made straight by moving your whole arm.

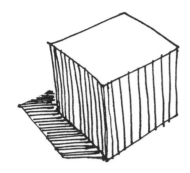

Figure 19

Figure 20

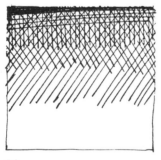

Figure 21

EXERCISE 10-4

Cross-Hatching
In your sketchbook use cross-hatching to indicate a range of tones from black to white as in Figure 21.

Shadow Shapes
In order to become more aware of what light, shade, and shadow do, notice the edges of the shadows on objects and faces. These edges are not always well defined, but for the sake of the next exercises draw them as if they were.

LIGHT, SHADE, AND SHADOW

The introduction of light, shade, and shadow to the drawing process can transform a simple two-dimensional diagram into an illusion of a three-dimensional form. If you want to use light as a means of enhancing the illusion of depth in a drawing, you must begin to observe what light does.

There are essentially three conditions of perceived light: one, a surface that is seen in direct light; two, a surface that is seen in shade because it is facing away from a light source; and three, the shadow cast on a surface by something blocking the path of the light. The conditions of shade and shadow will never be absolute because reflected light from other surfaces will lighten the darkness of the shade or shadow.

HATCHING AND CROSS-HATCHING

Hatching and cross-hatching can enhance the illusion of depth through the use of light, shade, and shadow.

Hatching consists of freehand parallel lines that give the impression of a tone of grey in an ink drawing, as in Figures 19 and 20. The closer the lines are to each other, the darker the tone; the farther apart and thinner the lines are, the lighter the tone.

There are many ways to apply hatching to rectangular forms. Here are two methods I teach beginning architecture students because they are simple to use and easy to remember.

Example 1: Use vertical hatching for shaded vertical surfaces, and horizontal hatching for shadowed horizontal surfaces as shown in Figure 19.

Example 2: Use a diagonal hatching that is not parallel with any of the edges. Use the same diagonal for all the vertical surfaces in shade. This will add consistency and unity to your drawing. Use horizontal hatching for the shadows on all horizontal surfaces as shown in Figure 20.

Cross-hatching consists of one set of parallel lines crossed by another set at a different angle as shown.

OTHER HATCHING SUGGESTIONS

Always use your eyes to tell where to hatch. When hatching a cylinder, such as a water tank or coffee cup, use vertical hatching. When hatching a sphere, use a curved diagonal hatching. Never use hatching and ink wash in the same drawing. The two don't work well together.

EXERCISE 10-5

Pen-Line Shading
Place an apple or pear on a white sheet of paper and place a desk lamp to one side and above the fruit. Draw the contour line of the fruit with your calligraphy pen, outlining the shade and shadow areas with a thin line. Diagonal-hatch the shaded areas and horizontal-hatch the shadow area on the table. Use fine lines.

EXERCISE 10-6

Pen-Line Shading
Place a slightly crumpled paper lunch bag under a desk lamp or in sunlight. Make a line drawing of the bag with your calligraphy pen, outlining the contours of the shade and shadow areas. Then apply hatching to these areas—diagonal-hatching for the lighter areas and cross-hatching for the darker areas. Use solid black in the places where the shadow is blackest.

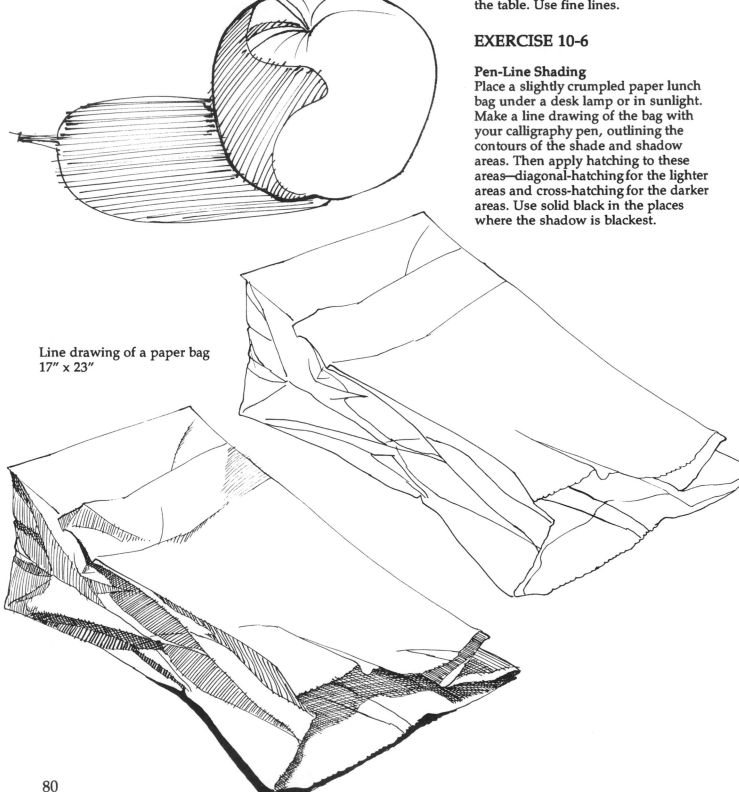

Line drawing of a paper bag
17" x 23"

80

Line and ink wash sample of a paper bag 17" x 13"

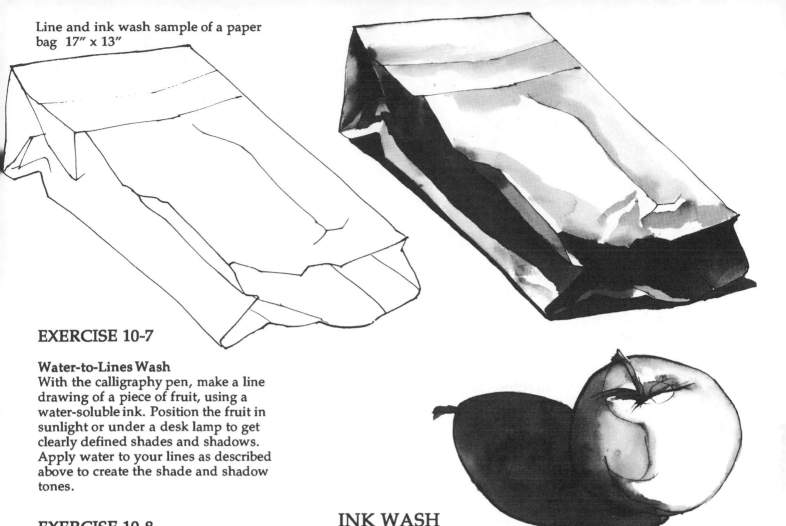

EXERCISE 10-7

Water-to-Lines Wash
With the calligraphy pen, make a line drawing of a piece of fruit, using a water-soluble ink. Position the fruit in sunlight or under a desk lamp to get clearly defined shades and shadows. Apply water to your lines as described above to create the shade and shadow tones.

EXERCISE 10-8

Premixed Ink Wash
First make an ink line drawing of a brown or white paper lunch bag positioned in sunlight or under a desk lamp so it has clearly defined shades and shadows.

Then mix a light gray ink wash as described above and apply it with the brush to your line drawing. Repeat with a darker wash and then with a very dark wash. Judge carefully according to your observation the lightness or darkness of each wash you apply.

It may be necessary to tip the paper one way or another to insure even application of your larger areas.

If one area is not dark enough, wait until it is completely dry before you add another wash to darken it. If an area is too dark, you can sometimes lighten it by applying clear water to the area and then removing the water with a thirsty brush. Do not blot your washes with a cloth unless you want an uneven texture.

INK WASH

A fast, easy way to apply shade and shadow to a drawing is by using ink wash. Ink wash is black ink diluted with water to produce various shades of gray. There are a number of ways to do this. Here are two:

Example 1: After the drawing has been made with the calligraphy pen and water-soluble ink, apply water with a brush to the side of the lines where you want the wash to occur. The black ink will follow the water to create a gray. Remove excess water with a thirsty brush—a wet brush that has been blotted with a rag. This is a very fast method to add shades and shadows to a drawing, but it can sometimes be difficult to control.

Example 2: After making the drawing with a pen or dry brush, mix your wash to the desired gray on a white saucer and apply it to the drawing with a brush. It takes only a small amount of ink to make a quantity of water gray. To make a soft edge, apply clear water to the edge of a washed tone before it dries. Beginners tend to make their washes too dark at first. Do remember, however, that ink washes usually dry lighter.

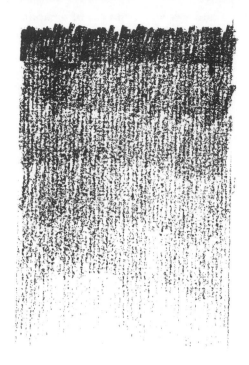

SOFT MEDIA

Soft drawing pencils, charcoal, and conte crayon are perfect drawing media for describing lighting conditions accurately. Shades and shadows are not often clearly defined and these softer media allow soft edges and subtle shading. The next exercises will acquaint you with pencil media and their potential. A Faber Castell, Design Ebony 6325 was used for the examples shown.

Figure 22

EXERCISE 10-9

Pencil Hatching
In your sketchbook make a hatching sample with a soft pencil similar to the one shown in Figure 22. Use a back and forth motion with the side of the pencil. Make the shading with diagonal strokes and let these strokes show. Work from the blackest black to the white of the paper, showing the full range of tone.

EXERCISE 10-10

Rough Pencil Drawing
Do a rough pencil drawing of an apple or pear in sunlight or under a desk lamp. Use contour pencil lines to define the fruit and the shade and shadow areas. Then apply diagonal pencil shading as you did in the previous exercise. Let your shading strokes show.

EXERCISE 10-11

Rough Pencil Drawing
Place a paper lunch bag under a desk lamp or in sunlight. First, draw the contours of the bag with your soft pencil. Next, draw the contours of the shade and shadow areas. Finally, apply diagonal-stroke pencil shading to these areas, letting your strokes show. Use solid black in the places where the shadow is blackest.

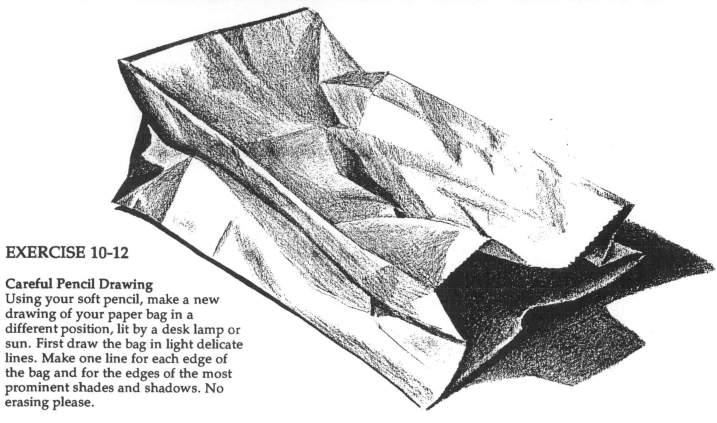

EXERCISE 10-12

Careful Pencil Drawing
Using your soft pencil, make a new drawing of your paper bag in a different position, lit by a desk lamp or sun. First draw the bag in light delicate lines. Make one line for each edge of the bag and for the edges of the most prominent shades and shadows. No erasing please.

Then carefully add the shade and shadow tones so the strokes of the pencil *do not show*. See how accurate you can be. Observe all the subtle changes in light and darkness. Shade right up to your contour lines so they blend with the shading and disappear.

When tones on different planes are close in value, emphasize one more than the other to distinguish them. Work to the full range of tone possible—from the blackest black to the white of the paper.

For a smooth soft quality, you can blend and soften the tones by rubbing them with your finger or a tissue.

EXERCISE 10-13

Careful Pencil Drawing
Light an apple or pear with a desk lamp or the sun. With a soft pencil make a contour drawing of the fruit on a sheet of textured or rough paper.

Observe and draw the contours of the shaded areas. Then shade these areas, using the full range of tone from black to white. Shade right up to the contour lines so they blend with the shading and disappear. Use your finger or a tissue to smooth and smudge your tones. This will soften your drawing and give it a finished look.

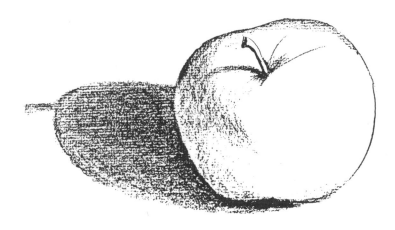

CONFIDENCE BUILDING

Many of the exercises in this chapter have required very careful observations and applications. One of the benefits of practicing drawing this way is that once you do it to your satisfaction, you will have proved to yourself you can do realistic drawing when you want to. This should give you the confidence to be even more creative and resourceful as you continue to learn, explore, and create other illusions.

84

11

Linear Perspective

There are many good books that give detailed rules for the use of perspective in industrial design, architecture, and interior architecture. But the best way to begin to understand perspective is to become aware of it experientially. If you try to understand rules and formulas before you understand the concept, you will just be confused.

AN EXPERIENTIAL APPROACH

We are going to treat perspective experientially in this book so you can understand it and apply its principles to your sketches of architectural subjects and other solid objects. It will be helpful if you can find a cube of wood to use as you are reading through this explanation. A child's building block will do. First let's understand the terms we will use.

Eye Level—Everything you draw on a paper is related to your eye level.

Horizon Line—Determined by your eye level or the eye level you want the viewer of your drawing to have.

Picture Plane—The plane of your picture is the sheet of paper you are drawing on. It can be thought of as a transparent window through which you are seeing your subject(s).

Vanishing Point—The point on the horizon line where straight parallel lines from the subject will vanish from view at infinity like a pair of straight railroad tracks.

Frontal Planes—Any plane that is perpendicular to your line of sight.

85

Longitudinal Planes—Any plane that is parallel with your line of sight.

Imagine you are flying an airplane and getting ready to land. From the window of the cockpit you can see the straight runway below you vanishing on the flat horizon. As you angle down the horizon goes above the window of the cockpit which corresponds to the picture plane.

At an altitude of a few hundred feet, the horizon comes into view again near the top of your windshield.

Now you are very near to the ground, perhaps only 25 feet off the ground. The horizon is lower in your window and the runway spreads wider and wider as you descend.

As you pull back on the throttle and the wheels touch the ground, the horizon appears very low through the windshield of the plane.

The horizon can be located anywhere. The higher its elevation in relation to your subject, the higher your viewpoint. This is what we call "a bird's eye view." The lower the horizon elevation, the lower your point of view. A very low horizon is used for what we call "a worm's eye view."

Horizontal parallel lines will vanish somewhere on the horizon line unless they are exactly perpendicular to your line of sight. In one and two point perspective, vertical lines will remain vertical.

When drawing perspective, always try to keep horizon lines and vanishing points away from the center of the sheet. This will insure that your drawing is not too symmetrical, and therefore, static and boring.

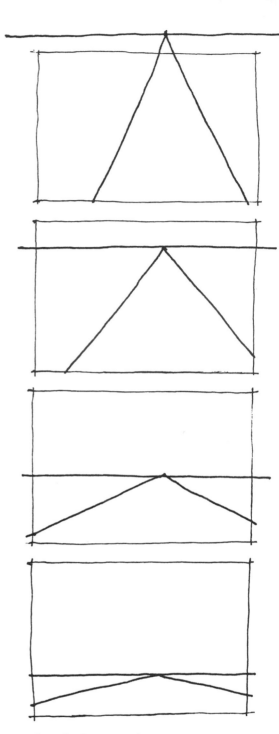

Simple diagram showing an airport runway as seen through the cockpit windshield of an airplane.

ONE-POINT PERSPECTIVE

Draw a horizon line across your sheet just above the center. Put a vanishing point on the horizon line somewhere to the right of center. Draw a square just below the horizon line and slightly to the left of the vanishing point. Draw lines from the vanishing point to the three nearest corners of the square. Now draw a horizontal and vertical line, as shown in Figure 23. The six horizontal and vertical lines represent the outline of a cube in one-point perspective.

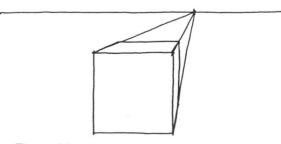

Figure 23

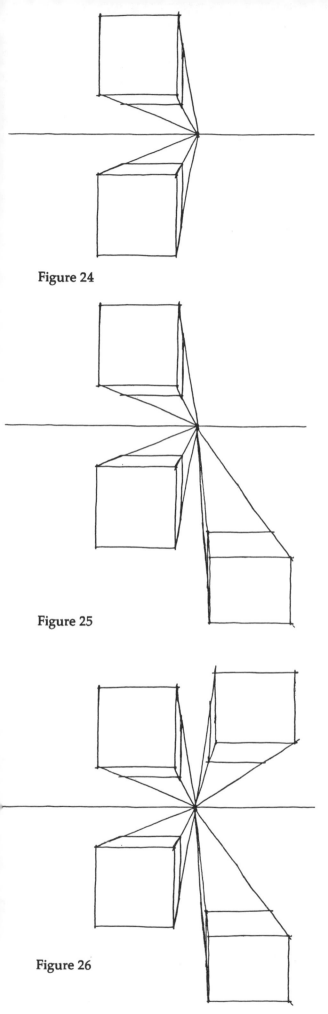

Figure 24

Figure 25

Figure 26

Pick up your wooden block. Hold it in front of you so you cannot see any of the sides. Then lower it just a little so you can see some of the top. Now move it to the left so you can see a little of the right side. This is what you have just drawn.

Now draw a cube above the horizon line, using the same vanishing point, as in Figure 24.

Pick up your wooden block and hold it so you cannot see any of the sides. Then lift it up so you can see a little of the bottom, and move it to the left so you see a little of the right side. This is what your above-the-horizon-line drawing represents.

Now lower your block so you see more and more of the top. You will notice that as it goes down you will see more top and less front. Now draw the block in the lower position on the right side of the vanishing point, as in Figure 25.

Lastly, raise the block once again above the horizon line, higher than before and to the right. You will notice that you see more bottom in this position. Draw it this way, as in Figure 26.

If you follow these directions, you should have a pretty good understanding of one-point perspective. If you are confused, go back and do everything again until you are confident. Do the following exercise before you go on to two-point perspective.

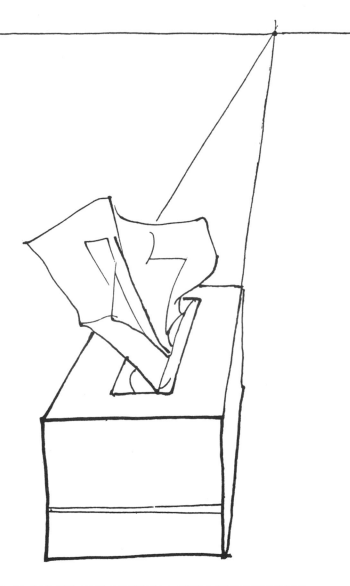

ONE-POINT INTERIOR PERSPECTIVE

Drawing an interior view of a room is just like standing inside your wooden block. You enlarge the block so that it fills your page. The vanishing points and horizon lines are now inside the block, as in Figure 27.

Draw a rectangle to represent the back wall of your room—the frontal plane. Decide how high or low your view is going to be and draw your horizon line at that height. Mark the vanishing point on the horizon line. Draw a line from this point to a corner of the rectangle (the back wall), and continue that line to the edge of the page. Do the same for the other three corners of the rectangle. Now draw the larger rectangle representing the outer limits of your room as shown. This will define the limits of the longitudinal planes—the floor, ceiling, and walls to your left and to your right. Remember to keep all the freehand vertical lines of your subject vertical.

EXERCISE 11-1

One-Point Perspective
Make a one-point perspective drawing of a tissue box, using your calligraphy pen. Put the horizon line and vanishing point on your paper in pencil before you begin. Organize your drawing using that information.

EXERCISE 11-2

One-Point Perspective of a Space
Make a one-point perspective drawing looking toward the frontal wall at the end of a long space such as a hallway, corridor, or alley. Lay out the perspective lines in pencil before you begin. Then make the drawing with your calligraphy or fountain pen.

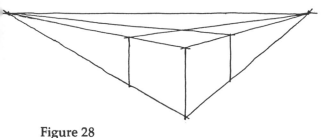

Figure 27

TWO-POINT PERSPECTIVE

Pick up your block and hold it with the front plane perpendicular to your line of sight. Now lower it so you see some of the top. The two edges parallel to your line of sight, if they were extended forward, would meet at the vanishing point on the horizon line.

Now if you rotate your block to the left, you will notice that point where these two parallel lines vanish on the horizon line will move to the left as well. As you continue to rotate it, you will notice you now have two more lines that will vanish on the horizon line to your right. This is what we call two-point perspective.

Figure 28

Take a sheet in your sketch book and draw a horizon line just above the center. Put a vanishing point near the left edge and one near the right edge on the horizon line. Now draw your block as shown in Figure 28. Be careful to keep your vertical lines vertical. After you have drawn your block in two-point perspective, compare your drawing with your block.

Now draw a two-point perspective of your block above the horizon line, as in Figure 29. Verify your drawing with your block.

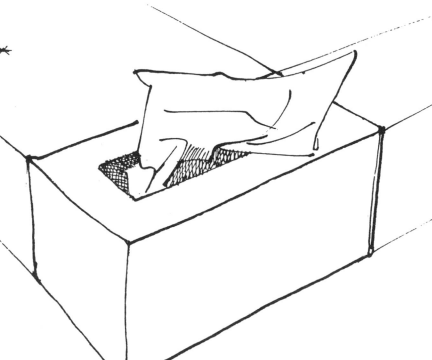

Figure 29

EXERCISE 11-3

Two-Point Perspective
Make a two-point perspective drawing of a tissue box, using your calligraphy pen. Locate the horizon line and vanishing points before you begin. Organize your drawing using that information.

GENERAL TIPS

Notice that in both one-point and two-point perspective, the far edges are shorter than the near edges.

Remember to check that the verticals of your subject are vertical in your drawing. You can do this by lining up the vertical with the edges of your paper.

In managing perspective, sometimes your subject will have vanishing points that are off the page. In that case you either have to set up points off the sheet or imagine that they are there. You can get pretty good at this with a little practice.

When drawing architectural subjects, always keep the perspective in mind. It is fine to draw without using perspective, but if you want buildings and rooms to look in perspective, it is a good idea to check your drawing as you work to make sure the perspective is correct. Always trust your eyes. Observe carefully and you will avoid perspective mistakes.

When tackling more complex buildings and three-dimensional rectangular subjects, reduce what you are seeing to cubes and multiples of cubes. If you can draw a cube in perspective, you can draw anything. Any rectangular subject can be simplified to its basic geometry.

EXERCISE 11-4

Two-Point Perspective
Make a drawing of an architectural subject. Take a view that is clearly a two-point perspective. Lay out your guidelines— horizon, vanishing points, and main lines of the drawing—in soft pencil. Complete the drawing with your fountain or calligraphy pen.

90

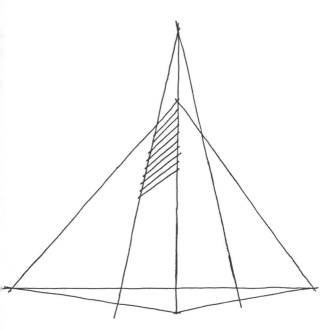

Figure 30

THREE-POINT PERSPECTIVE

Three-point perspective simply means that there is a third vanishing point for the vertical lines. Three-point perspective is usually used to show a dramatic view looking up or down at a subject. We use three-point perspective when we draw tall buildings from the ground looking up (as in Figure 30) or from an airplane looking down (as in Figure 31). The vertical lines, instead of being vertical, will converge to a point in the sky or earth. Locate your third vanishing point where you think it belongs according to your eye. It may occur off your sheet of paper. Learn to work from imaginary points on and off your paper.

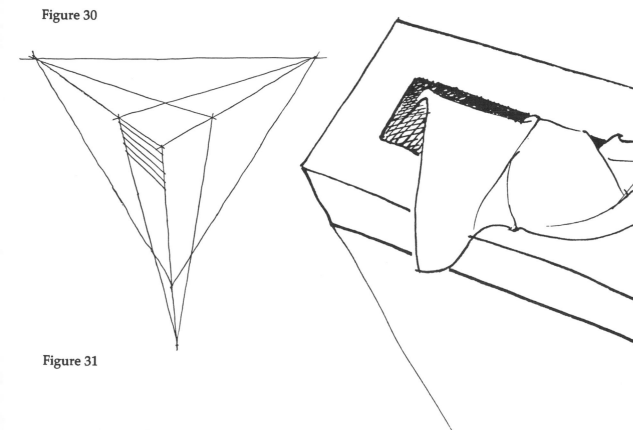

Figure 31

EXERCISE 11-5

Three-Point Perspective
With your calligraphy pen, make a drawing of a tissue box that is sitting on the floor. You will be looking down at it from your chair. Notice how the vertical seem to converge underground somewhere. Before you begin, use light soft pencil lines to align the vertical edges to the vanishing point.

ELLIPSES

Being able to draw a good ellipse takes practice, but is extremely useful. All sorts of wheels, coins, bottles, jars, glasses, vases, and circular architectural subjects such as domes, windows, and arches will require drawing ellipses.

Ellipses can always be reduced to a square to make drawing them easier. For example, take the wooden block you have been using. Pretend you have turned it into a cylinder. Draw the block first in one-point perspective, then make it into a cylinder. Notice when it is below the horizon line, the bottom curve will be more open than the top. Always be careful when drawing the bottom ellipse of a cylinder. This is an important fact that must be observed.

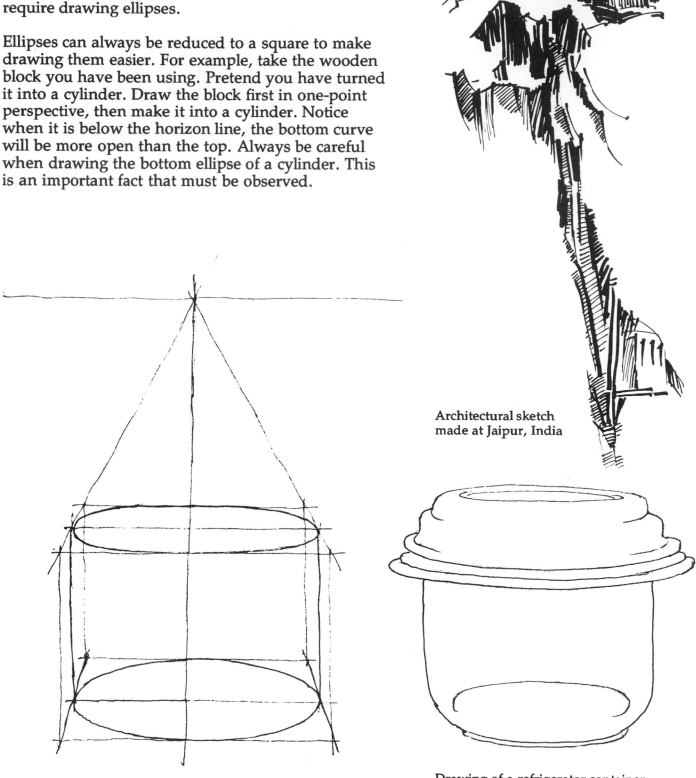

Architectural sketch made at Jaipur, India

Drawing of a refrigerator container using the diagram on the left as a guide for drawing the ellipses.

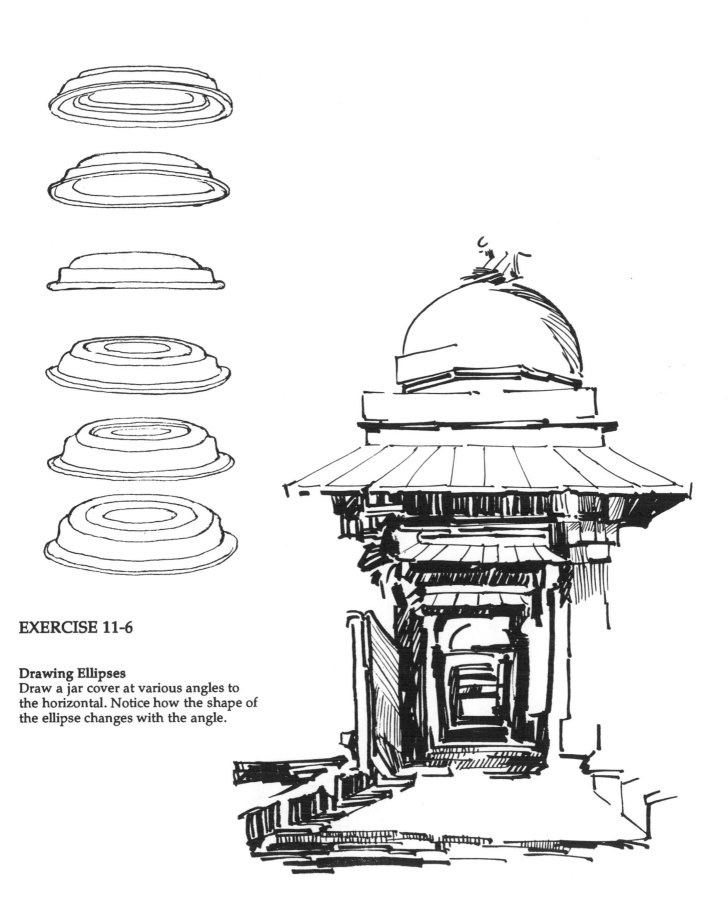

EXERCISE 11-6

Drawing Ellipses
Draw a jar cover at various angles to
the horizontal. Notice how the shape of
the ellipse changes with the angle.

Calligraphy pen sketch of an exterior
passageway at Fatepur Sikri, India

Bamboo pen and ink drawing
24″ x 18″, 2 minutes

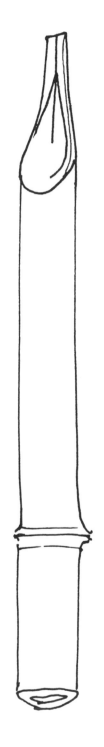

Homemade bamboo pen
with a chisel point

12

More Applications

Here are some ideas to stimulate your creative expression. These exercises will help you to let go and draw with increased freedom and added technical skill.

BAMBOO PEN

Bamboo pens are available in most art stores, but it is also easy to make one if you can find the bamboo. Look for a stalk that is from ¼" to ½" in diameter and is fairly dry (yellow in color). Do not use a green stalk. Cut a piece about 10" long. Fashion the point as shown with a sharp knife well away from a joint as shown.

If you make your own pen you can fashion the chisel point, which is much more versatile than the points that come on commercially available bamboo pens. The chisel point will give a thick and thin line. If you buy a bamboo pen with a sharp point, you can easily modify it to a chisel point with a pocket knife or a nail clippers.

Draw with this pen both when it is wet with ink and when it is almost dry. When wet it will deposit a lot of ink on the paper, which makes it a great instrument for the water-to-line wash technique.

Water-soluble ink line with clear water
added for toning 17" x 14", 7 minutes

FACE IN THREE-QUARTERS VIEW

In seeing and drawing the face in a three-quarters
view, it is a good idea to become aware of a few
differences. In a front view the face appears as an
oval, but in three-quarters it will be considerably
wider. The distance from the top of the head to the
chin will be about the same as the distance from the
forehead to the back of the head. The eye that is
farthest away from you may appear a bit smaller.
The distance from the eye nearest you to the chin
will be the same as from the nearest eye to the back
of the ear.

Bamboo Pen Drawing with Wash
With your bamboo pen, make a check-
back contour-line drawing of a person's
face. Use a desk lamp or outdoor
sunlight to obtain clear shades and
shadows on your subject. With the
brush and clear water, describe the
shades and shadows of the face by
touching the contour lines with the wet
brush. Watch the water-soluble ink flow
into the water. Use plenty of water.

Allow accidents to happen. If the wash
gets too dark or too watery, remove the
excess with a thirsty brush (rinse the
ink out of the brush and dry it on your
rag; then the damp brush will be
thirsty, like a damp sponge, and will
soak up the puddles of water from the
paper). Don't forget to record your
experience at the bottom of each
drawing.

Three-quarters view made with a
calligraphy pen 17" x 23", 10 minutes

EXERCISE 12-2

Face in Three-Quarters View
Using your calligraphy pen, make a
detailed three-quarters-view drawing of
a face. Pay attention to the relative
dimensions of the head. Work large on
the sheet. Let the head fill the page.

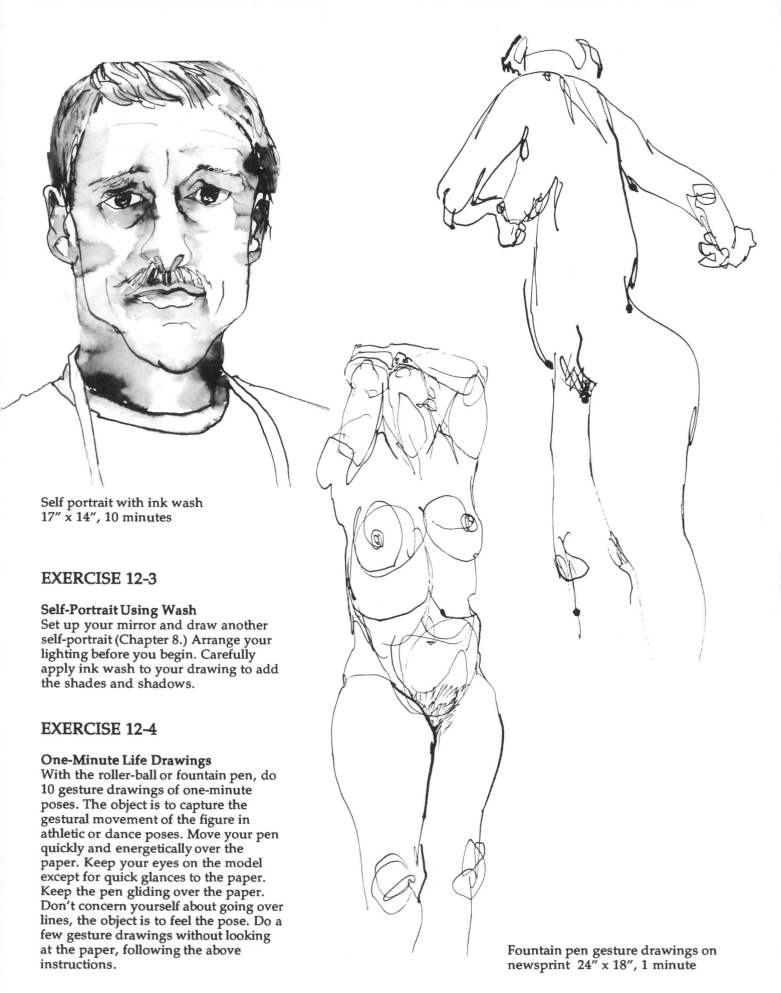

Self portrait with ink wash
17" x 14", 10 minutes

EXERCISE 12-3

Self-Portrait Using Wash
Set up your mirror and draw another
self-portrait (Chapter 8.) Arrange your
lighting before you begin. Carefully
apply ink wash to your drawing to add
the shades and shadows.

EXERCISE 12-4

One-Minute Life Drawings
With the roller-ball or fountain pen, do
10 gesture drawings of one-minute
poses. The object is to capture the
gestural movement of the figure in
athletic or dance poses. Move your pen
quickly and energetically over the
paper. Keep your eyes on the model
except for quick glances to the paper.
Keep the pen gliding over the paper.
Don't concern yourself about going over
lines, the object is to feel the pose. Do a
few gesture drawings without looking
at the paper, following the above
instructions.

Fountain pen gesture drawings on
newsprint 24" x 18", 1 minute

DRY BRUSH

A dry-brush drawing has the looseness and freedom of a charcoal drawing, and the permanence of ink. It is fast and easy once you get the feel of it. A dry brush is prepared by first wetting the brush with water and then filling the brush with black ink. I recommend the Higgins nonwaterproof india ink or a good quality Chinese or Japanese ink.

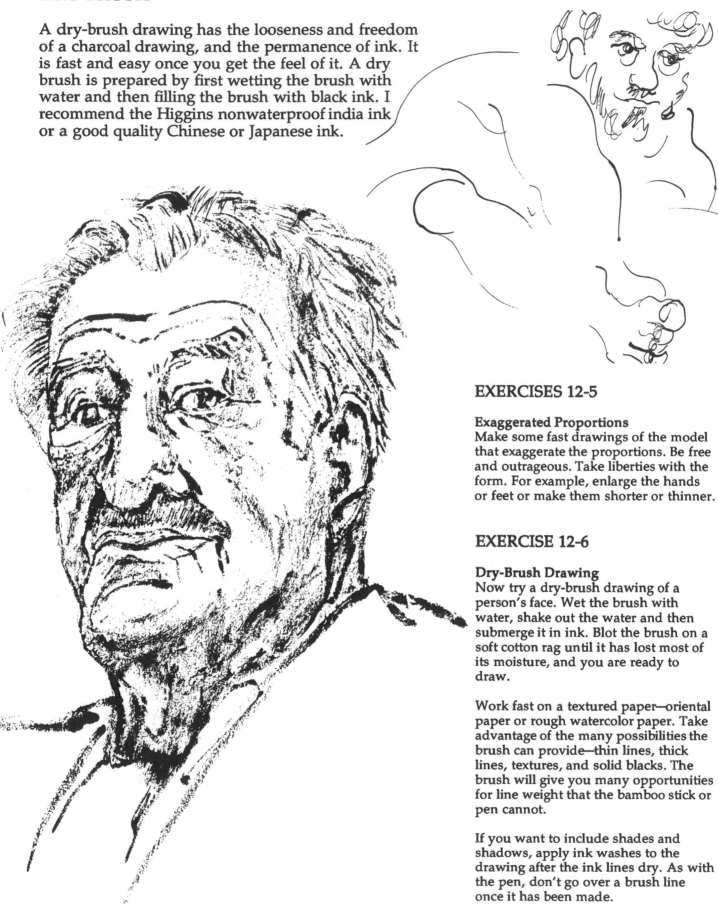

EXERCISES 12-5

Exaggerated Proportions
Make some fast drawings of the model that exaggerate the proportions. Be free and outrageous. Take liberties with the form. For example, enlarge the hands or feet or make them shorter or thinner.

EXERCISE 12-6

Dry-Brush Drawing
Now try a dry-brush drawing of a person's face. Wet the brush with water, shake out the water and then submerge it in ink. Blot the brush on a soft cotton rag until it has lost most of its moisture, and you are ready to draw.

Work fast on a textured paper—oriental paper or rough watercolor paper. Take advantage of the many possibilities the brush can provide—thin lines, thick lines, textures, and solid blacks. The brush will give you many opportunities for line weight that the bamboo stick or pen cannot.

If you want to include shades and shadows, apply ink washes to the drawing after the ink lines dry. As with the pen, don't go over a brush line once it has been made.

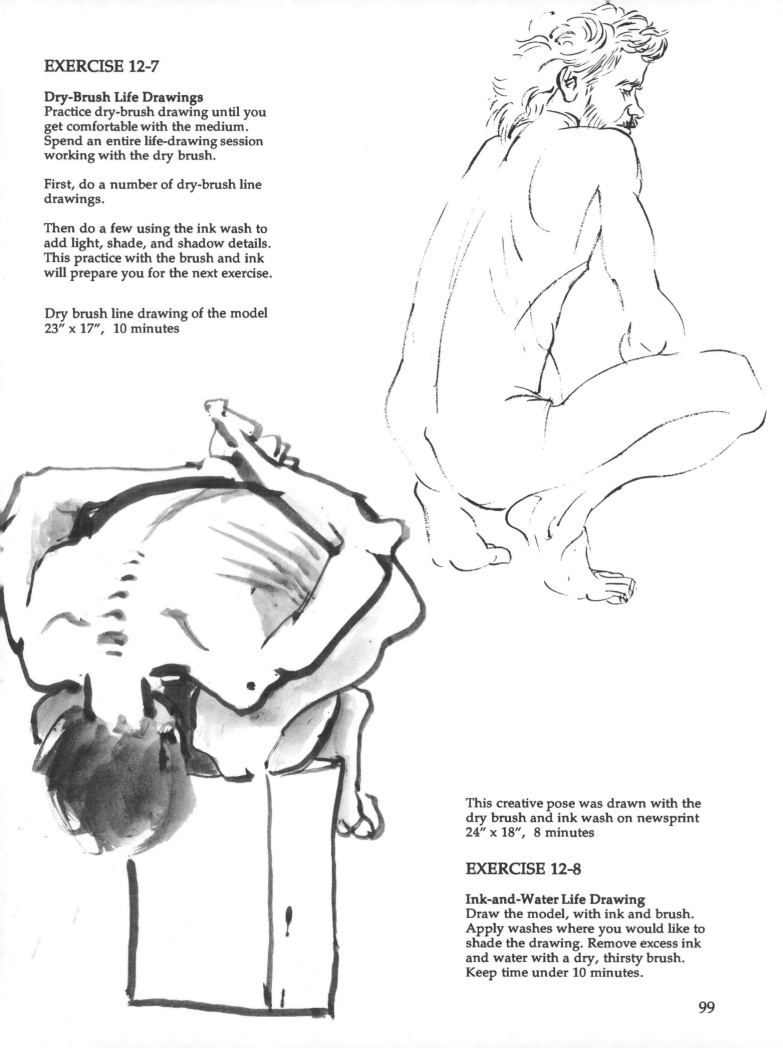

EXERCISE 12-7

Dry-Brush Life Drawings
Practice dry-brush drawing until you get comfortable with the medium. Spend an entire life-drawing session working with the dry brush.

First, do a number of dry-brush line drawings.

Then do a few using the ink wash to add light, shade, and shadow details. This practice with the brush and ink will prepare you for the next exercise.

Dry brush line drawing of the model 23" x 17", 10 minutes

This creative pose was drawn with the dry brush and ink wash on newsprint 24" x 18", 8 minutes

EXERCISE 12-8

Ink-and-Water Life Drawing
Draw the model, with ink and brush. Apply washes where you would like to shade the drawing. Remove excess ink and water with a dry, thirsty brush. Keep time under 10 minutes.

Long-stick demonstration

EXERCISE 12-9

Long-Stick Drawing
Cut a bamboo stick at least three feet long. Put your ink bottle on the floor next to your pad of paper. Standing over your paper, do a drawing of the model. Hold the stick near the end.

These drawings can be very strong and free. This is a very liberating technique. You may surprise yourself with your accuracy. Allow 8 to 10 minutes for each drawing.

Long-stick drawing
24″ x 18″, 8 minutes

100

EXERCISE 12-10

Life Drawing and Hatching
Make a line drawing study of the figure
with your fountain or calligraphy pen.
Then apply diagonal hatching for the
shades and shadows.

Pen line drawing with hatching added
17" x 14", 6 minutes

EXERCISE 12-11

Water Life Drawing
With your brush, draw the figure with
clear water first. Use plenty of water.
Then using the bamboo stick or pen,
apply ink lines over the water contours
you have drawn. Wonderful accidents
will occur as you do this. This exercise
requires a free and accepting attitude.
The results can be exciting or
devastating. Be ready for both.
Experiment with this technique often. It
can help you to let go, relax, and have
fun.

Clear water drawing with ink line
added with the bamboo pen or stick
23" x 34", 10 minutes

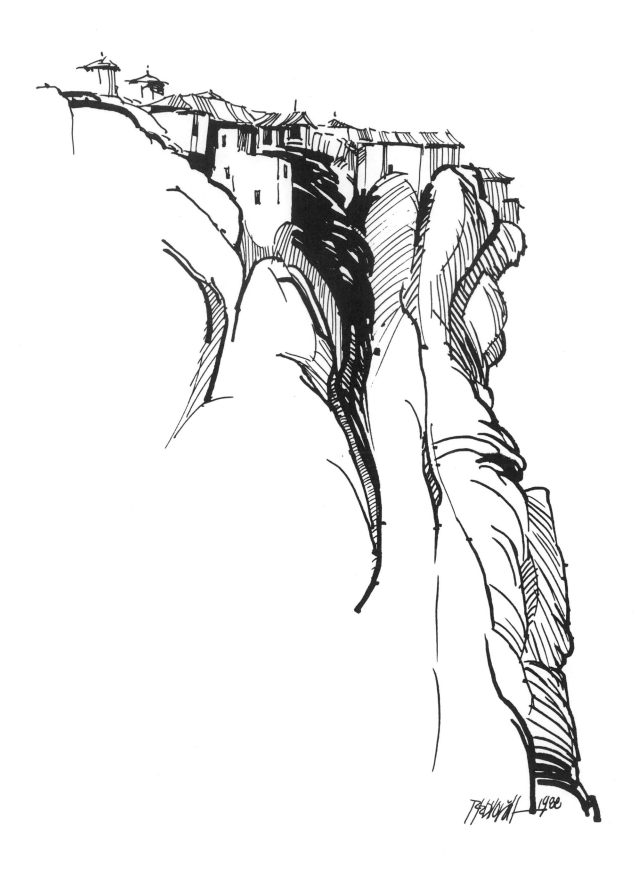

PART
III

THE REWARDS

*Our duty as men (and women) is to proceed
as if limits to our ability did not exist.
We are collaborators in creation.*
        --Pierre Teilhard de Chardin

In Part III we are going to apply our creativity and
explore our world with imagination and insight. If
you have followed the course so far, you have
learned to really let go and immerse yourself in the
drawing process. You are now going to learn how to
appreciate and talk about drawings. We will make
some creative inquiries and enjoy more of the
rewards of Experiential Drawing.

13

How To Talk About A Drawing

Most people don't know how to talk about a drawing. They look at a drawing as a judge. They decide whether a drawing is successful or not by how well it represents the subject drawn. However we have learned that drawing is more than representation. Drawing is a personal experience. Representation can be a desired option, even an intention, but it certainly isn't the only purpose.

When we look at a drawing we can ask such questions as: Was the artist enjoying him or herself? Was the investigation—the visual exploration—a thorough one? Do the lines indicate a clean and direct approach? Can we see spontaneity, life, and movement in the drawing? Does the composition intrigue, inspire, delight, frighten, move, amuse, or please us?

OPINION

We must remember that any time a person comments on a drawing, it is only an opinion that is being expressed. Since drawing is a creative and subjective activity, everyone experiences and appreciates a drawing in a different way, from their own point-of-view.

UNDERSTAND

Look at the drawing. What do you understand about it? For example, what medium was used? What was the subject? What do you think was the intention of the artist? Was it done quickly, or was it a labored drawing? Does it help us see something in a different way? For example, from that person's point-of-view, do you think the artist was trying, consciously or unconsciously, to say something? If so, what was the message?

REMIND

What does the drawing remind us of? Does the style remind us of another artist's style? Does the drawing remind us of a place, an object, a person, or an experience? Travel sketches are great reminders. They recall a time and place from a vacation or foreign land.

Drawings can remind us of sports we love. They can remind us of our children at a certain age. Self-portraits can remind us of the way we looked when we did the drawing. All drawings remind us of something.

WHAT DO YOU SEE?

When you look at a drawing, ask yourself, "What do I see?" What you see and what someone else sees may be different. You see a subject, but you also see lines— dark lines, light lines, moving lines, poetic lines. You see space—composition, light and dark, shades and shadows. You see scale and balance, or imbalance. You see the placement on the piece of paper, the emphasis, and perhaps you even see what the artist intended you to see.

EXPERIENCE

What is your experience while you look at the drawing? What do you think was the experience of the artist? Is there a clear reference or is there obscurity? Do you think the artist enjoyed making those lines? Was the artist really looking carefully—exploring his subject?

Tower Fall, Yellowstone National Park
Calligraphy pen and wash, 5 1/2" x 17"
(double page sketch book drawing)

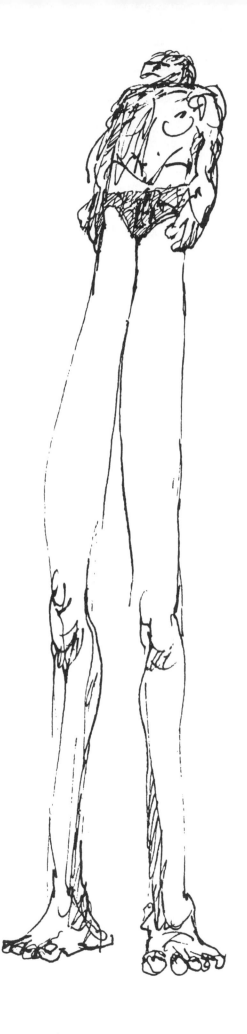

EXCITEMENT

Does the drawing excite you? Can you tell if the artist was excited when he was creating the drawing? Can you see energy, emotion, and life in the drawing?

ENTHUSIASM

There is an expression, "Enthusiasm sells." When you look at this drawing, can you feel the enthusiasm of the artist? Had the artist let go, was he or she at play? Or was the artist working hard, even suffering, as he or she produced this work?

LIKES AND DISLIKES

In your personal opinion, what do you like most about this drawing? What is it that grabs your attention? How do you respond? Do you like the way it is drawn? Is there anything you don't like about the drawing? Is the drawing upsetting or disagreeable?

Sometimes the artist wants to communicate a strong idea or feeling. The drawing may have been done in order to move people to action against some injustice the artist feels. There is nothing that says a drawing must be agreeable or beautiful. Rembrandt's drawings of the crucifixion tell a morbid story. Political cartoons will, in a powerful way, convey the artist's political opinions and convictions. Medical drawings can portray surgical procedures.

On the other hand, drawings can be uplifting and inspiring. They can motivate us to positive feelings and actions. Drawings in children's books can be fanciful or descriptive.

FEELING

How does the drawing make you feel? Do you get pleasant or sad feelings? Does the drawing upset you, anger you, or frighten you? Are you sharing in the artist's feelings when you look at the drawing?

JUMPING OVER THE MAGIC LINE

These are some of the many ways to talk about a drawing other than as a judge. The viewer who only judges misses so much experience.

When you talk about a drawing, jump over the magic line. Leave your rational, critical thinking and get up to your experience, to your creative expression—spontaneous, nonjudgmental seeing.

Mom's Hands
This drawing was made of my mothers hands during a visit.
Calligraphy pen, 17" x 14", 12 minutes

EXERCISE 13-1

Talk About a Drawing Practice
Practice talking about the drawings illustrated on this page and the next. Look at each drawing from the points of view that have been discussed and share your experience of them with your class or another person.

EXERCISE 13-2

Talk about a Drawing
Pair up with a friend. Each of you select one of your drawings you feel particularly good about sharing. (I suggest you begin with one of your head and face drawings for this exercise.) Take turns going through the above list and talk about each drawing. It is important that when your partner talks, you listen without answering back. When you talk, your partner should listen without answering back. If there are any additional comments or discussions you would like to have, take a few minutes to do that at the end of your exchange.

This is a great exercise to do in class or out. It is extremely rewarding and validating. Both partners will finish the exercise feeling better about themselves and their drawing. It takes a lot of creativity to talk about a drawing in this way. You will be richer for the experience.

Drawing of Earl Payne
Earl took my Experiential Drawing class
and I used his face to demonstrate the
bamboo stick. I talked with him after
class and then wrote the following on
the drawing. *"Drawing of Earl Payne,
the old salt, fought in the Spanish Civil
War, drank scotch with Ernest Hemingway.
His face, glass eye and all, tells of a life well
lived. He 'took the road less traveled
by'—tough as nails with a heart of gold.
XII-8-1985"*
Bamboo stick on oriental paper
17" x 14", 10 minutes

Redondo Beach Road, Chinese ink on
oriental paper 14" x 19" 14 minutes

14

The World Around You

In this chapter we will look at a myriad of ways to look creatively at the world around us with more opportunities to enjoy the drawing process. Remember, your experience is the most valuable focus. Here are suggestions on finding drawing experiences for fun, excitement, perhaps even some mischief. Here are some challenges, creative ideas, and rewards.

Pen drawings of a wooden chair. The drawing on the left was the preliminary pencil layout; on the right the finished drawing. 23" x 17" 1 hour

CHAIR

When I was considering going to architecture school, a wise architect friend of my family gave me a test. He said that if I passed the test I would have what it takes to graduate from architecture school. The test was to go home and draw a wooden chair in pen and ink and bring it back and show it to him.

I fulfilled my assignment. I did a number of drawings from different angles of a wooden chair. He gave me a passing grade, not so much for the quality of my drawings, but more for just having followed through with the assignment.

He was right, I did graduate from architecture school. If you can follow through with the next exercise, you can draw anything.

In order to do chair drawings you will need to recall what you have learned about perspective. You will also need a chair. I prefer an old wooden one.

EXERCISE 14-1

Wooden Chair Drawing
Make a drawing of a wooden chair in your 18" x 24" sketch book with your fountain pen or your calligraphy pen. Begin by drawing the chair in pencil. Make perspective guide-lines to assist your accuracy. Remember, a chair is built around a cube shape.

Then draw right over your pencil lines with the pen and ink. This can be a time-consuming exercise. It may take as much as an hour to complete your drawing, depending on the complexity of your chair. Take your time and really get to know your chair.

112

EXERCISE 14-2

Chair Space
With your pen, do an overlay of your chair drawing to indicate the negative space around the chair (see Chapter 7). A variation on this exercise is to blacken the space around the chair. Then the chair space will appear as if the chair has disappeared and left a white void.

EXERCISE 14-3

Drawing of a Shoe
Draw one shoe with clean calligraphy pen lines. Draw it double size. Put the shoe on the paper before you begin and mark off the double length with two small pencil lines.

Begin by carefully drawing the laces. Now is your chance to use the overlapping planes illusion. Put in all the details. Draw the thickness of the leather and fabric. Stitching is applied with dashed lines, an important detail.

Detailed calligraphy pen drawing of a child's running shoe
17" x 14" 15 minutes

SHOES

Shoes are an ideal drawing subject. They have numerous details to discover and explore. I have collected boxes of old shoes—running shoes and my children's outgrown shoes—to use in my drawing classes. Children's shoes communicate so much. They are memories of past days at play; of feet that were once little; of feet that were once learning to walk.

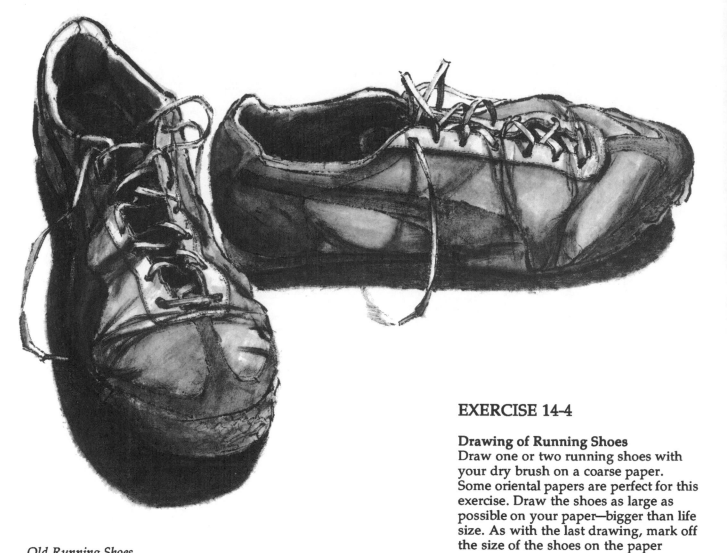

Old Running Shoes
Ink, dry brush, and watercolor on
oriental paper 36" x 42" 3 hours

EXERCISE 14-4

Drawing of Running Shoes
Draw one or two running shoes with
your dry brush on a coarse paper.
Some oriental papers are perfect for this
exercise. Draw the shoes as large as
possible on your paper—bigger than life
size. As with the last drawing, mark off
the size of the shoes on the paper
before you begin. Draw the overlapping
laces first. Finish with dry-brush
shading.

EXERCISE 14-5

Combination Drawing of Shoes
On a table, arrange an assortment of
shoes from your closet. Light them with
a desk lamp or the sun. With dry brush
or calligraphy pen, draw your "shoe
still life." Take the time to put in the
details—laces, stitching, sole patterns.
Then add the shades and shadows with
ink wash mixed and applied from a
saucer. Work as large as possible.

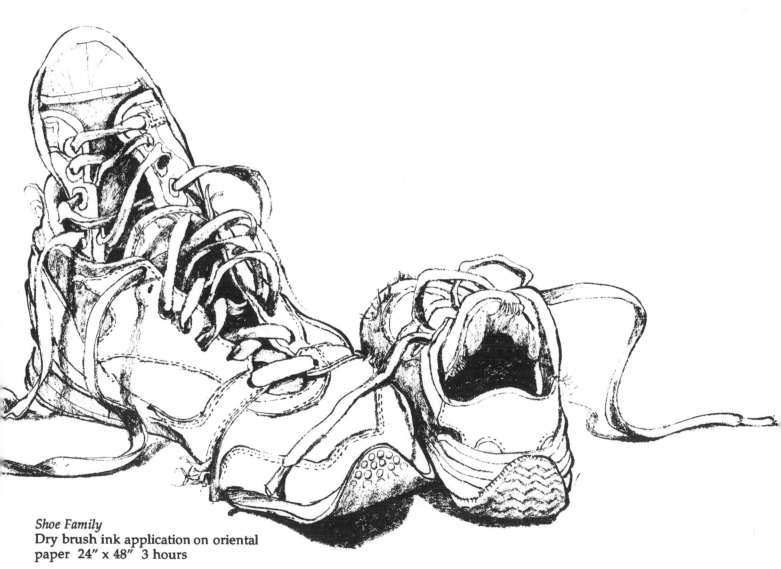

Shoe Family
Dry brush ink application on oriental
paper 24″ x 48″ 3 hours

Calligraphy pen drawing of a Calla Lily
23" x 17" 6 minutes

EXERCISE 14-6

Flower Drawings
Do a series of flower drawings over a period of days. Draw a variety of flowers. Begin with interrupted contour-line drawing. Then try adding ink wash. Work larger than life.

Try budding flowers and wilting flowers as well as blooming flowers.

Calligraphy pen and ink wash
17 x 14" 6 minutes

FLOWERS

Flowers are another great drawing subject. I have spent hours at local nurseries and flower stores drawing flowers. Most people who sell flowers are willing to let you sit in the shop for an hour or two and draw if you come at a time when they are not too busy. You will be a novelty in the shop—you must be prepared to answer questions and listen to comments about your drawings.

Flowers require a lot of attention to overlapping planes. First, draw the parts of the flowers and leaves that are closest to you.

PEOPLE IN PUBLIC PLACES

Drawing people in public places—in parks, libraries, restaurants, on trains or planes, at the theater—is a real challenge. You must get used to the idea that your subjects will not sit or stand still. Be ready to abandon a drawing when someone moves away. But the anticipation of a sudden change in your subject's posture will motivate you to work fast. It is excellent training and will keep you loose.

If you want to remain undiscovered, draw people from enough distance that they won't notice you are drawing them. If someone notices you drawing, he/she may want to see what you have done. Depending on how you have drawn him/her, this may or may not be a wise idea. My advice is to remain obscure.

Remember that a person drawing in public is like a magnet. People who don't draw love to watch. It is better than a magic show because it is not a trick, it is really happening. If you are going to draw in public, be ready to encounter onlookers. Most people will not bother you if you look like you are really concentrating. And if you are, you will not have time to pay attention to the fact that you are being watched.

EXERCISE 14-7

Drawings of People in Public Places
Carry a small pad of paper and a fountain pen with you. When you find yourself in a public place with time on your hands, draw. See how long it takes you to fill a sketch book. Draw every chance you get. When you get home, remove and discard any drawings you don't like.

ANIMALS

Animals are a challenge to draw, especially at the zoo. But what an experience it is to learn about animals as you draw them. Take a medium-sized sketch pad to the zoo with you and spend the day drawing. Work with fast, continuous lines at first. The animals are constantly moving, even when they are asleep, so you must work fast.

I recommend a fountain pen or roller-ball pen so you won't have to find room for a bottle of ink. A portable stool will make the day more pleasant. If you can, go on a weekday when it is not crowded. Discard all the drawings you don't like, but wait until you get home. Your drawings may look different to you when you get home, or even the next day.

Sketch of a wild rabbit
6 1/2" x 8 1/2" 3 minutes

EXERCISE 14-8

Animal Drawings
Draw your bird, dog, fish, rabbit, cat—whatever pets you have. Sometimes it may take 10 or 20 drawings for you to get one you like. Work with your pens brush, and pencil. Try dry brush, wet brush, wash, pencil shading.

Go to your nearest zoo, spend a morning or afternoon drawing. Work fast with your pens. Do a variety of animals— birds, cats, reptiles, etc. Make your drawings as large or small as you desire.

Fast drawing of a lion
at the San Francisco Zoo
6 1/2" x 8 1/2" 30 seconds

Calligraphy pen sketch of a female lion
5 1/2" x 15" 6 minutes

Quick sketch made at the elephants at
the San Francisco Zoo
6 1/2" x 8 1/2" 1 minute

EXERCISE 14–9

Old Cars
Do a number of drawings of old cars or
trucks. You can use the vehicles
parked on your own street. Work with
pen and hatching or pen ink and wash.

OLD CARS

Old cars are a great drawing subject. They have
many details that newer cars don't have. The more
details you have to work with, the more fun your
drawing experience can be. Spend the day drawing
old cars at the next concourse show near you. Take a
small portable stool with you so you can sit while
you work. You will have a great experience and meet
lots of wonderful people.

Drawing of a Pierce Arrow made at a
family picnic 14" x 17" 20 minutes

LANDSCAPES

In the United States we enjoy some magnificent landscapes. A visit to any national or state park will inspire you with opportunities to draw and test your sense of composition. You will need to use all your technical knowledge and observation skills when drawing the landscape. The trick in landscape drawing is knowing what to leave out and developing quick methods to represent distant views—water, hills, mountains, trees, and sky.

TREES

Trees come in many different shapes and forms. Your goal is to capture the essence of the tree. It is not necessary to draw every single branch, twig, and leaf. With practice, you will discover shorthand representations that give the illusion of different trees and tree parts.

Trees are made up essentially of five elements: roots, trunk, branches, twigs, and leaves or needles. They are also made up of masses of textures and patterns. If you keep these elements in mind when you draw, your trees will be more convincing.

EXERCISE 14-10

Neighborhood Trees
Pick out favorite trees in the area where you live. Sketch them separately and in groupings. Make some tree sketches using hatching and cross-hatching for shade, shadows, and foliage textures.

120

EXERCISE 14-11

Ink-Wash Trees
Do a series of trees using ink-wash to describe the light and dark of the trunk, branches, and foliage.

EXERCISE 14-12

Dry Brush Trees
Next try some drawings made with the dry brush. Use a very dry brush for the foliage. Fan the brush, dip the bristle ends into the ink and then draw the trunk and branch bark textures.

EXERCISE 14-13

Tree Roots
Do a series of studies of tree roots. Make one study with ink line and wash. Do another of tree roots using the dry brush technique. Fan your brush for bark textures.

Detail from a larger dry brush drawing 12" x 32"

Ink and wash drawing
12" x 17" 8 minutes

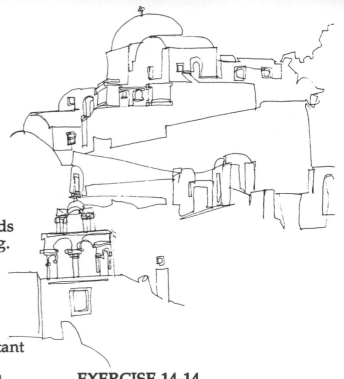

Santorini Architecture, two continuous-line contour sketches
8 1/2" x 11"   3 minutes each

ARCHITECTURAL SUBJECTS

Architecture makes a good subject because it stands still. The only thing that will change is the lighting. All kinds of architectural subjects are available—houses, churches, state capitols, bridges, monuments, temples, and any other man-made structure around the world.

In drawing architecture, probably the most important consideration is selecting what you are going to draw. Select subjects that will attract your eye and inspire your hand. Draw what interests you or excites you. Draw those subjects you want to experience visually and as intimately as you can.

When beginning to sketch architecture, it is a good idea to pick subjects that not only interest you but also are manageable to draw. Subjects that are too complicated or too intricate in detail will frustrate and discourage you. Barns are a good beginning architectural subject. Their forms are fairly simple and easily described in line. As you gain confidence drawing architectural subjects you can try more complicated compositions.

Other good subjects are buildings from a distance—buildings in the landscape, houses on hillsides, harbor views from passenger and cruise ships, and aerial views of urban subjects. Keep your drawing small, and the detail you need to include will be minimal.

As you gain skill, attempt more challenging subjects. When drawing any subject, the enthusiasm you are feeling at the time will communicate through the drawing. When you increase your enthusiasm for your subject your drawing will come alive.

Sometimes a knowledge of your subject will create a deeper understanding and empathy. For example, while traveling, read a guidebook that informs you about architectural subjects, or take a tour in which the subjects are explained to you. When you draw those subjects, your newly acquired knowledge will make that experience more meaningful for you.

EXERCISE 14-14

Architecture - Contour Drawings
Begin architectural subjects with a continuous-line blind contour. This will get you relaxed and focusing on your subject. When doing these drawings, remember to draw your verticals vertical. This is often a problem for persons starting to sketch architecture.

The next step is to make continuous-line drawings using the check-back method.

Finally, work with interrupted lines and add hatching.

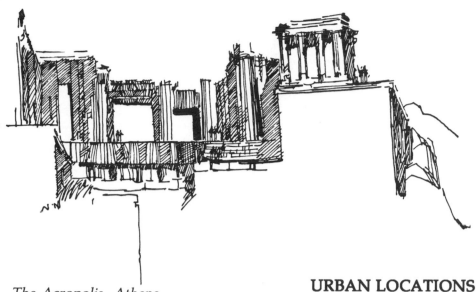

The Acropolis, Athens
8 1/2" x 11"   12 minutes

Old Town, Warsaw
Calligraphy pen sketch
8" x 10"   10 minutes

URBAN LOCATIONS

When drawing exterior views of buildings and other architectural monuments, it is important to select the view you are going to take before you begin drawing. Don't just sit down anywhere, but take the view you find most interesting. If your subject is in a large city, you must situate yourself where you will have a minimum of distractions.

The drawing may take anywhere from 10 to 45 minutes to complete. If you're located on a busy street with people walking in front of you all the time, your task is nearly impossible. Sometimes you can find a place to draw that is quiet and relaxed; for example, indoors looking out through a window. Tea rooms and cafes, indoor and outdoor, can provide that kind of protected atmosphere.

A handy device to carry with you is a small fisherman's stool that folds up and can be carried easily in a small day-pack along with your sketching materials. This will allow you the flexibility to sit and draw anywhere you desire.

Calligraphy pen drawing of Naxos, a Greek island harbor, drawn from the deck of a passenger ferry on a scrap of bristol board
3 1/4" x 4 3/4"   2 minutes

Clarence
Pencil on textured paper
17" x 23" 20 minutes

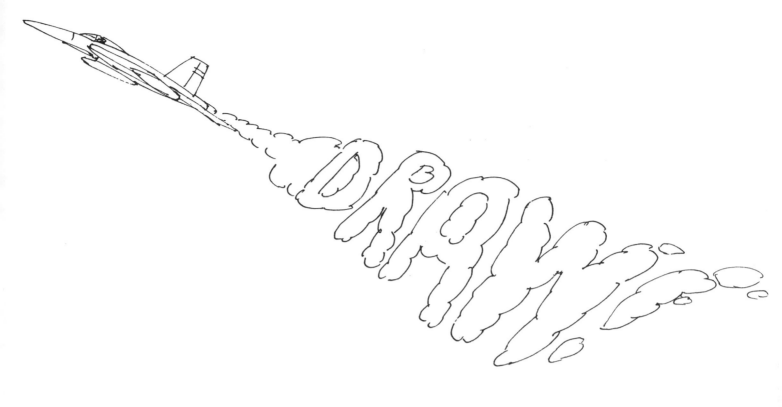

15

Drawing For The Joy Of It

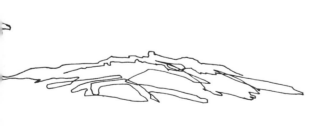

Like life, Experiential Drawing is a journey, not a destination. If you have followed the text and exercises in this book, you are well on your way to personal discovery. You have learned that the Experiential Drawing process can make you more aware of your visual world. It will bring your subjects together with your personal objectives. In short, the purpose of drawing is drawing.

If the process of drawing is a relaxing, fulfilling activity, then the resulting images, the evidence of your experience will demonstrate that. Every time you begin a drawing, you take a new risk. Even with a subject you have drawn many times, the latest drawing is always the newest challenge.

GETTING IN TOUCH

Let your creative self show in your drawings. Let drawing help you get in touch with problems, beliefs, and deep feelings you have about your life and the world. Express your fears and joys as you work. Sketch out your problems. Draw with the feelings you have about events, people, places, and things.

Draw yourself from different points-of-view. Draw how you are feeling right now. Represent yourself as you see yourself. Make a drawing of you, drawing yourself, in a full-length mirror.

Acknowledge your creative self as an artist. Think like an artist. Let drawing be a part of your life, like a mirror, microscope, or telescope that helps you see

Drawing can guide you through difficult periods. It can help you honor and acknowledge friends and relatives at celebrations—birthdays, marriages, and anniversaries. You can draw your pains and discomforts. A friend and student told me that drawing helped her to manage her chemotherapy cancer treatments. She said it was the only thing she could do during that difficult time. Another friend told me that drawing helped her maintain her sanity when she lost her young son.

DRAWING FROM PHOTOGRAPHS

I don't recommend using photographs as a primary source for material to draw. However, a black and white photograph can be used to help study light and dark values. Sketch from photographs the same way you would from life. Pencil drawings are particularly appropriate for capturing photographic tones.

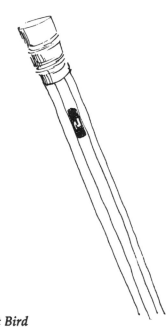

Photographs can make available material that would ordinarily be out of the question. For example, if you want to draw celebrities—sports figures, movie stars, or political figures—photographs may be your only opportunity. Photographs can also help you draw animals and figures in motion, a very difficult task to accomplish from memory.

The Smallest Bird
**Drawing made from a photograph
in the June 1990 issue of
National Geographic magazine
11" x 14"   15 minutes**

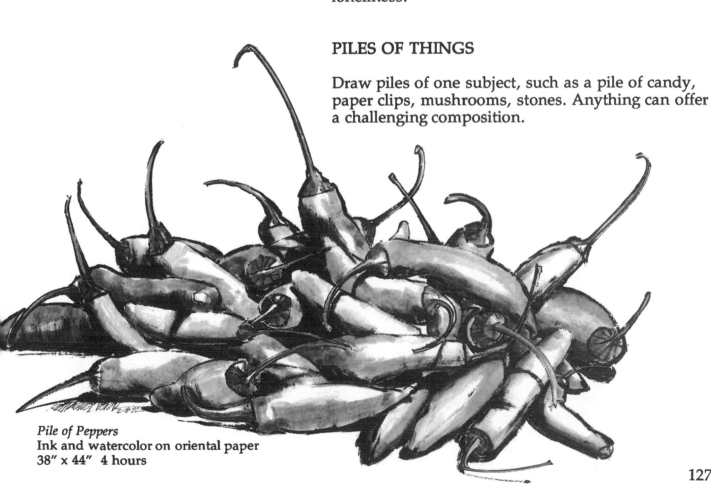

Cajun singer, sketched from television
11" x 14" 1 minute

TELEVISION

Drawings can also be made from the TV screen. The best sources are programs that show the same images many times like talk shows, interviews, and musical productions. Drawing from moving images on TV can be very challenging and exciting. Because of the speed required to work with this kind of material, there is no time to think, only to create.

ENVIRONMENTS

Drawing can bring you in touch with your living environment. You can draw interior views of your living spaces. I had a friend who did a lot of traveling abroad. He showed me sketchbooks in which he had chronicled each room where he had spent the night on his travels.

Another artist I know uses the stationery of the hotel where she stays when she travels to sketch the people and places she sees.

Andrew Wyeth has made many drawings and paintings of empty rooms and solitary figures in empty rooms, a repeating theme of isolation and loneliness.

PILES OF THINGS

Draw piles of one subject, such as a pile of candy, paper clips, mushrooms, stones. Anything can offer a challenging composition.

Pile of Peppers
Ink and watercolor on oriental paper
38" x 44" 4 hours

UNLIMITED POSSIBILITIES

The possibilities for inventive exploration through drawing are infinite. Use your eyes. Discover and explore. Put the familiar together with the unfamiliar, the large with the detailed, the small with the microscopic. Make big from small and small from big. Draw with enthusiasm, energy, and excitement as your eyes search the multitude of possibilities.

CONCLUSION

The purpose of Experiential Drawing goes beyond the mere ability to record images on paper. The process of Experiential Drawing can make you more familiar with your inner world—your world of conscious awareness. In this book you have discovered ways to validate your creative experience and increase your conscious awareness. You have learned to explore and discover intimate detail—to observe carefully. You have discovered new ways to see and create.

Continue to be curious. See with an open mind and a sense of humor. Draw for the experience of it. Draw to see, to create, to understand yourself better, and your relationship with the world.

Experiential Drawing is a present-time experience. It is at its best when it is a spontaneous act, done without too much thought and consideration. Let it be simply a bubbling up of the creative energy that lies within each of us.

There is a story of a famous landscape painter in a small village in Japan. One day a young man asked him if he would do a painting of a fish for him. The artist agreed to do it. During the course of the next year, the man asked the artist if the painting was finished. Each time he was given the same reply: "I'm still working on it."

The young man left the village and went to the city. He became a very successful businessman. He returned to the village rarely, and only for short visits to his family. He forgot about the painting.

Being
Pencil drawing
36" x 25"

128

Twenty years went by. Then one day on one of his short visits, he ran into the painter on the street. He remembered his request and asked the painter if he had ever completed the painting. The artist said, "Come with me." He took the man to his house. He served the man tea, as was the custom.

While the man was sipping tea, the artist laid out a sheet of white paper on his painting table. He ground some black ink on his ink stone, picked up his brush, and proceeded to paint a fish. In a few minutes, the painting was finished.

The artist beckoned the man to come and see what he had done. When the businessman observed the painting he was so overcome with emotion that he dropped his tea cup and tears rolled down his cheeks. For a few moments he was speechless. In this painting of the fish he saw not just the image of a fish, but the struggle of the fish to swim upstream to the place of its birth where it would spawn its offspring. He saw the struggles of his own life and the awareness of that most important moment of all of life, *now*.

The man exclaimed, "It is absolutely beautiful. It is beyond words." And then in astonishment he said, "And it took you but a few minutes to complete!" Then he asked the artist, "Why didn't you paint this for me twenty years ago when I asked you?"

The artist led the man to a storage room. The businessman saw many five-foot-high stacks of paintings—hundreds of paintings of fish. The artist said to the man, "Your painting took twenty years, and a few minutes, to complete.

It is my wish that you have begun an exciting journey that will occupy your creative endeavors for years to come. Please don't be impatient for a certain kind of result. Appreciate what you are doing now. Value the experiences you create for yourself.

Enjoy drawing!

APPENDIX

Working With A Model

TO THE INSTRUCTOR

Here is a technique for getting exciting poses. Before each pose, give the model a verb to act out. The pose will then originate from the model's creativity and direct experience of that activity.

This technique gives the model the opportunity to express his or her own self on the model's platform. The model feels that he/she is participating on a much higher level than just simply assuming a posture and holding it. The model is posing from the inside out. The model gets excited, the students get inspired.

Here are some of the verbs I have used: holding, driving, climbing, stretching, dressing (can be done with clothes), walking, pushing, pulling, eating, reading, playing baseball, playing tennis, dancing, playing music, crying, being sad, yelling, being worried, fighting, relaxing, sleeping, feeling great, working, studying, riding, building, feeling proud, feeling pity, being excited, listening, seeing for the first time, recognizing, bossing, asking forgiveness, talking on the phone, scolding, doing aerobic movements, feeling frustrated, being alive.

Always be courteous and respectful of a model's privacy and comfort. The instructor and students should be the only people permitted in the room, and the room is closed to outside viewers. The model will need a private place to change before and after the session. Keep the room warm enough for an unclothed person. If you feel it is necessary to touch to get a desired posture, it is imperative to ask permission first.

I believe in using a 50-50 balance of male and female models. Many art teachers prefer the female; however, I feel it is important to work with both sexes. The male can offer additional challenges and variety. I consider it a privilege to work from a live model of either sex.

Introduce the model to the class before you begin, and acknowledge the model in front of the class when the session is over. Students usually feel a strong sense of gratitude for the model's work. Voice these sentiments for the class.

FOR THE MODEL

The best models work at creating alive vital poses for the people who are drawing. A good model has a strong influence on the success of a drawing session. A poor one will be hard to work with and the students will feel cheated. Many models are artists themselves and understand the needs of the students.

The best attitude for a model is a willingness to please the instructor and the class. Although most life-drawing sessions have little verbal communication with the model, there is still communication with body language and energy. Here are some tips for a model to remember.

1. Be friendly, and have a willing and positive attitude. Ask the teacher for instructions and special requests before the session begins. If there is a break, ask how you are doing and if the instructor has any suggestion.

2. Be willing to change or alter a pose if asked by the instructor.

3. The best poses are the ones that look alive and natural. Sometimes a twist of the head or body can transform a pose from acceptable to exciting.

4. Remember that the pose you assume will play a major role in the success of the student's experience.

5. Do not be shy about showing certain parts of your body. Your self-consciousness is embarrassing to the students. A model who is willing to be open and flexible, face any direction, and use their body to create any posture, is appreciated.

6. Think of your body as sculpture. Think of each pose as a living sculpture you are creating.

7. While you are posing, think what you will do for the next pose. Then you won't waste valuable class time searching for the right posture.

8. Use good balance. You will be able to do incredible things with your body just by establishing a strong balance and a steady foundation.

9. Use props - hats, scarves, poles, or other items—to provide variety and creativity to the session. Before using props, however, clear that option with the instructor.

10. Don't be afraid to challenge yourself. Let your model session give you opportunities for muscle toning and stretching. For short poses, do action postures you could not hold for the longer poses.

11. Come to the session bathed and clean.

12. Always arrive a few minutes early to get instructions and allow changing time.

13. Have your own timer. Take responsibility for timing each pose. A little digital timer with a beeper will work great. Counting is all right, but not as good, because sometimes you can forget what number sequence you are on.

14. Be sure and rotate your poses so you will face every student during the session.

15. Do not carry on conversations with the students while you are posing unless the students have initiated the conversation and it is clearly all right with the instructor that you do so.

16. Provide a balance of standing, sitting, and lying poses if no request has been made.

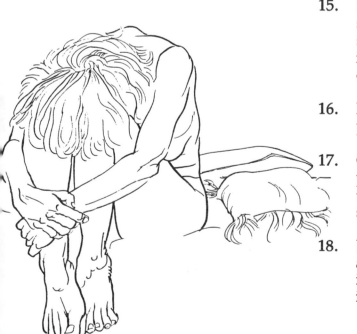

17. Give the students 15 to 30 seconds to turn their pages and prepare for the next pose. Take that time yourself to get the circulation moving and stretch any tight muscles.

18. Be inventive and creative. Think of yourself as an artist at what you are doing. Pose from the inside out. This will make the session more interesting and pleasant for you.

CREDITS

P. 7
Student unknown, *Profile*, These two drawing were made by an adult woman during a one day drawing class at Monterey Peninsula College, Monterey, California. She brought the drawings to the author after class. He copied them and gave them back to her.

P. 18
Olivia Cherion, *Shoe*, These three drawings were made by Olivia Cheriton when she was in first grade, age 6, on 9" x 12" drawing paper with a black felt marking pen during a 45 minute drawing class presented by the author. The three drawings have been reduced for reproduction.

P. 19
Owen Ellickson, *Running Shoe*, These three drawings were made by Owen Ellickson when he was in third grade, age 8, on 9" x 12" drawing paper with a black felt marking pen during a 45 minute drawing class presented by the author. The three drawings have been reduced proportionately for reproduction.

P. 21
Elli Sandis, *Running Shoe*, These two drawings were made by Elli Sandis when he was in the 6th grade, age 11, on 9" x 12" drawing paper with a black felt marking pen during a 45 minute drawing session presented by the author. The two drawings have been reduced proportionately for reproduction.

P. 72
Vincent Van Gogh, *Cypresses Under Night Sky*, (Lost: This drawing disappeared during the Second World War) India ink drawing made with a reed pen 18 1/2" x 24 1/2", Kunsthalle, Bremen.

Rembrandt van Rijn, *Christ Washing the Disciples Feet*, Ink drawing, Rijksmuseum, Amsterdam.

Tatsuo Saito, *Squirrel on a Grape Vine*, Private Collection, Tokyo.

Pablo Picasso, *23-6-68*, The Art Institute, Chicago.

P. 73
Albrecht Durer, *Demonstration of Perspective, Draftsman Drawing a Line*, Woodcut, 4 1/4" x 7 1/3" Kupferstichkabinett, West Berlin.

Leonardo da Vinci, *Detail from notebooks*, Source unknown. Reproduced from personal file notes.

All other pages:
Robert Regis Dvořák created all the other drawing examples in this book.

BIBLIOGRAPHY

Arnheim, Rudolf, *Art and Visual Perception*, Berkeley and Los Angeles: University of California Press, 1966.

Blake, Vernon, *The Way To Sketch*, New York: Dover Publications, Inc. 1981. (This is an unabridged republication of the 1929 edition published by Clarendon Press, Oxford)

Carroll, Lewis, Illustrated by Steadman, Ralph, *Alice In Wonderland*, New York: Clarkson N. Potter, Inc. 1973.

Chaet, Bernard, *The Art of Drawing*, New York: Holt, Rinehart and Winston, Inc. 1970.

Dodson, Bert, *Keys To Drawing*, Cincinnati: North Light Books, 1985.

Dvořák, Robert R., *Drawing Without Fear*, Palo Alto, California: Dale Seymour Publications, 1987.

Dvořák, Robert R., *The Pocket Drawing Book*, Menlo Park, California, Inkwell Press, 1986.

Edwards, Betty, *Drawing on the Right Side of the Brain*, Los Angeles: Houghton Mifflin Co., J. P. Tarcher, 1979.

Frank Frecerick, The Zen of Seeing, New York: Vintage Books, 1973.

Goodrich, Janet, *Natural Vision Improvement*, Berkeley: Celestial Arts, 1985.

Green, Barry with Gallwey, Timothy W., *The Inner Game Of Music*, New York: Doubleday, 1986.

Hanks, Kurt, *Draw*, Los Altos, California: Crisp Publications, 1977.

Klee, Paul, *Pedagogical Sketchbook*, New York: Frederick A. Praeger, 1967.

McKim, Robert H., *Experiences In Visual Thinking*, Monterey, California: Brooks/Cole Publishing Co. 1972

Nicolaides, Kimon, *The Natural Way To Draw*, Boston: Houghton Mifflin Co. 1975.

Perls, Frederick, *Gestalt Therapy Verbatim*, Lafayette, California: Real People Press, 1969.

Samuels, Mike and Samuels, Nancy, *Seeing With The Mind's Eye*, New York: Random House, Inc., 1975.

ROBERT REGIS DVOŘÁK

Drawing on a rich background of life experience, painting, traveling, sailing, teaching, music, and an interest in psychology, Dvořák has been teaching drawing to adults and children for 25 years. Since 1976 he has been giving one and two day Experiential Drawing workshops. In 1989-90 Dvořák was awarded a grant from the California Arts Council to promote art to elementary school teachers and children.

Raised in a musical midwestern family he received his undergraduate education at the University of Illinois then moved west for a graduate degree from the University of California, Berkeley. From 1970-72 he was awarded the Rome Prize and became a Fellow of the American Academy in Rome. Dvořák was a professor of architecture for seven years at the University of Oregon and two years at the University of California, Berkeley, where he taught design, problem solving and visual communication skills including drawing, film, painting, and other media communication skills. He has traveled extensively and at various times could be seen making caricatures in Japanese night clubs and Greek tavernas, sketching on the Great Wall of China, drawing temples in India, making watercolors of windmills in Holland or painting waterfalls at Yosemite National Park.

Dvořák's workshops on drawing, watercolor, and creative thinking promote personal awareness, inspire imagination, vision, and risk taking. He has written and illustrated four books: *Drawing Without Fear, The Pocket Drawing Book, Productivity at the Workstation,* and *Experiential Drawing;* produced 23 posters of his drawings, paintings, and woodcuts; and made 22 short 16mm films. Many of Dvořák's paintings and films are in corporate and private collections.

If you have enjoyed this book you will be pleased to learn that CRISP PUBLICATIONS specializes in creative instructional books for both individual and professional growth.

Call or write for our free catalog:

CRISP PUBLICATIONS, INC.
1200 Hamilton Court
Menlo Park, CA 94025

(800) 442-7477